THE GREAT PYRAMID MYSTERY

New Discoveries Revealed

By Stephen Stuart Douglas

Corn Collection Picture Discovered in Ancient Egyptian Tomb

"Always a popular subject, The Great Pyramid of Giza in Egypt is fully explained. Discover it for yourself! Who, What, Where, When, Why and How it was built. This book is the first serious pursuit in nearly a century of the famous Seven Year Famine connection to the Great Pyramid Mystery. All the facts and figures in this book have been carefully researched. Get ready to be amazed, the most mysterious building in the world is about to become a popular topic of discussion and documentaries; Again!" Author

This work is lovingly dedicated to my Dad & Mom: Mr. Stuart & Helen Douglas of Maryland.

Photographs by Mr. Rob Golding of Maryland & Mr. Ted House of Ohio, diagrams by Author;

Additional thanks to my Lovely Angela Marie and son Noah Spencer Douglas, also friends: CreateSpace Publishing, Fern Abbott of Ohio, Eric Anderson of Ohio, Mr. Jeff Ayers of Maryland, American Hero & Author Heath 'Colonel Bo' Bottomly of California, also Trucker Bruce Banks of New York City and Mississippi, Sis Ruth Dillon of Maryland, Bro James Douglas of Maryland, Historian & Author Deborah Richmond Foulkes of North Carolina, Rob Golding, Ted House, Trucker Bob Hale of South Carolina, Jerry Hutto of Mississippi, Author Jimmy James of Texas, Trucker Bob Midgett of Kentucky, Trucker Kenneth Quincy of Ohio, Mr. Tom Rolcik of Kentucky, Wayne & Linda Smith of Ohio, 'Farmer' William Temple of Ohio, Sis Susan Thacker of Maryland, Mr. Todd Ward of Indiana, Trucker Jim Wynn of Kentucky, fellow members of the Clan Douglas Historical Society, my Church friends, all my Facebook friends and everyone that enjoys Egyptian History.

Table   of   Contents

"Tribute To Khufu" SSD

I am climbing up the great stone steps, level by level I climb,
looking out across the plateau, at a beautiful sunrise sublime.

The burning Eye of Ra, soon to ascend up far higher then I,

bright yellows, oranges and reds, coloring the morning sky

The desert below, of rocks and sand and clustered palms,

and long lines of people hard at work, singing tribal songs

My family of old hath been chosen to rule, by God and by men this is true,

who dare wag the head, who dare turn the back or play the rebellious fool

Peace to you my friends, peace too you my enemies, know that I have won,

seven years of plenty have passed , seven years of great famine have come.

I am climbing up the great stone steps, level by level I climb,
finally reaching it's summit, listen to the African wind chime.

I AM KHUFU! I shout out, my voices echoing about, surely you hear me,

I AM PHARAOH! I shout, who can doubt, between earth and sky and sea

Behold my Silo, Behold my Tomb, of life and death I hold the key,

Behold my Tower, Behold my perfect Pyramid, marvelous for to see

Four thousand years and more I shall lay here entombed, waiting for that day,

when future Egyptians shall discover my secret room, where my treasures lay

For now, I shall climb down the great stone steps, level by level I shall climb,

knowing this Great Pyramid shall be a wonder, enduring to the end of time.

INTRODUCTION: A NEW THEORY TAKES SHAPE

"History is shy and loves to tease, especially ideas preconceived" SSD

The Great Pyramid of Giza has always fascinated me. How exciting it is to read a book or look at a picture or watch a documentary about it. Like so many others, possibly yourself included, I also pondered the wonderful mysteries of this Pyramid as a thought hobby. After pursuing many of the popular theories to their ends, I reasoned upon some interesting ideas. Finally I began to investigate these in earnest. Through the fun of research and discovery this unexpected new idea materialized. By the end of the year I was writing this book.

When you have found the right answer to a problem, suddenly all the different parts fit together. The following combination of thoughts started the direction of my mind toward a pivotal connection between The Great Pyramid of Giza and the Biblical story about a Seven Year Famine. The idea was ridicules but every new discovery confirmed that unlikely connection. The more I looked for a piece of the puzzle that would not fit the more I recognized the right answer may have finally been re-discovered as all the pieces of strangely shaped facts fit together perfectly. Recent discoveries and ancient rumors seem to have united.

First in these thought experiments was the Sphinx. The ancient Sphinx could be one of the keys to solving the mystery of The Great Pyramid. It seems to have been built about the same time as The Great Pyramid. I was never one to think it was a religious symbol. Curiously it is situated directly front and left of the Pyramid's door facing away toward the Mediterranean Sea and the land of Canaan, not honoring the dead Pharaoh but as if welcoming visitors, exactly as it does today. But the Great Sphinx on the Giza Plateau is situated well inside Egypt's natural border and The Great Pyramid itself was sealed shut to friends and visitors alike. Still the Sphinx is facing away from the ancient land of Egypt. The Sphinx is shaped with its wide head and long body as to shade adults during the day and even invite children to play on it. In fact the whole body of the Sphinx bares a lot of wear markings not consistent with nature's wear and tear. Another oddity is the human face on an animal's body, opposite from Egypt's later representations of animal heads such as a bird or crocodile on a human body. Most Egyptologist conclude the face on the Sphinx was that of Pharaoh's Sneferu or his son Khufu or Khafre, whom are also believed to be the most likely builders of the Giza Pyramids. A narrow beard was once attached to the chin of the Sphinx which is another clue it was the face of a Pharaoh, since most ancient Pharaohs had warn narrow chin beards. Like the American Eagle offering both the olive branch of peace or the arrows of war, so Pharaoh has the lions body of fierce power yet is reclined peaceably. It represented to me the mighty nation of Egypt with Pharaoh as head. It seems to be a national civil symbol rather than religious. It was an ancient statement, a symbol, a landmark, maybe a gathering point.

Second of these considerations was the antiquity of this period in history. Human history this far back in time consist of few limited facts glued together with many professional interpretations. I was never one to accept that the First Kingdom Pharaohs or many of the Old Kingdom Pharaohs styled themselves as gods on earth, nor had they fashioned a pantheon of images to worship as the later Pharaohs clearly did. I believe the limited facts support the idea of Strong Kings and Lords of "Birthright", among lesser Nobles, Crafters and Peasants. Egypt was probable the first real Nation (in the modern sense of the word) on Earth and they accomplished it the same way many others would in the evolution of human society, a Royal House uniting many Noble Families from many city-states and towns by marriage, diplomacy and brute force to form a single Nation. The word Pharaoh means "Great House of Egypt". Later Dynasties would cultivate the divine status of Pharaoh and the religious evolution of Egypt. But the fantastic wealth and monuments of Giza already present would continue. Such a display of super wealth did not appear in Egypt till The Great Pyramid of Giza was completed, encased with interlocking granite slabs and golden cap. To me this Pyramid represents a seismic shift in human history, something new and bold with sudden unimagined wealth. I began to suspect the new wealth and the very idea that a Pharaoh King could become a god on earth may have been the unintended result of so many thousands of people visiting one single place.

Third, The Great Pyramid has been an attraction for all of the modern age and in differing degrees all the ages of common writing. It is not a big leap to suppose such a monument would not have always been a curiosity and commonly known landmark since it was first built in long ago antiquity. I could easily understand that the unique interior design would be forgotten in a generation or two and even the builders name lost. Yet the basics of the project and the purpose must have been common knowledge for a very long time. History can be changed in the retelling but such an imposing monument cannot be denied. Its purpose must have been recorded in ancient text and story without mention of its particular shape. The story would be Egyptian and Monumental, maybe even Biblical.

Finally fourth of these considerations, the mysterious Shafts passing through the structure of The Great Pyramid must be a final key to solving the mystery. The Shafts are unique to anything ever discovered in antiquity. After applying them to one function after another, I decided they could only have served one practical use. This brought me back to the familiar seven year famine story from ancient Egypt describing many of the exact same details unique to The Great Pyramid. The coincidences were suspect because The Great Pyramid was missing the required space needed inside and the two events were dated hundreds of years apart. Pursuing further to assure myself that it was an impossible link, I found the apparent missing link. It was simply amazing! All the pieces were already there and making this connection suddenly fit them together! Hence this book "The Great Pyramid Mystery" solved.

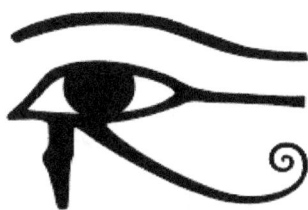

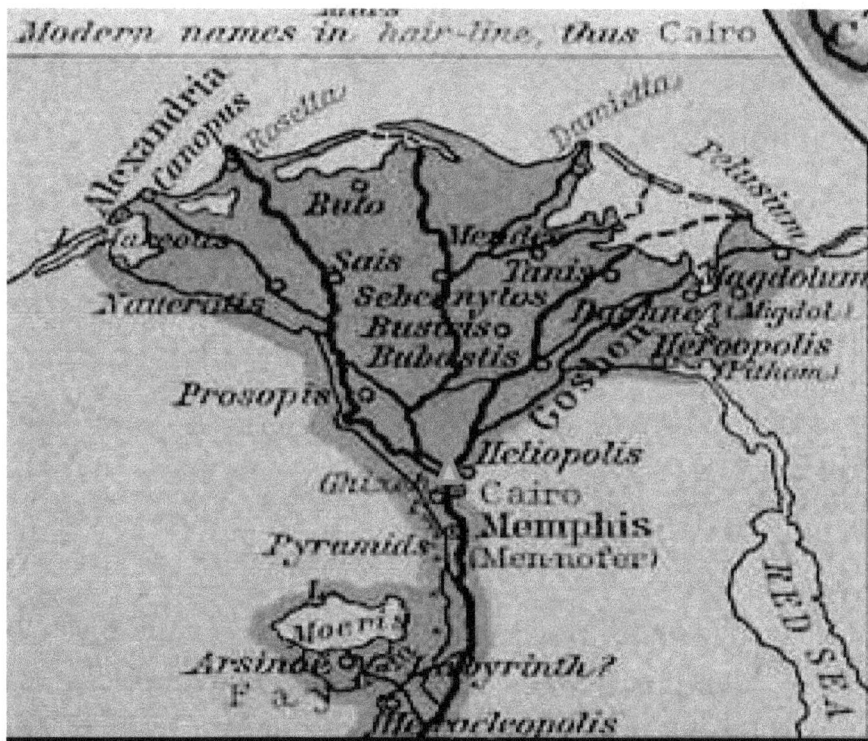

Modern names in hair-line, thus Cairo

CHAPTER ONE   UNIFING THE MYSTERIES:

"With the lack of a confession the circumstantial evidence must be compelling" SSD

Part One = MYSTERY

The Great Pyramid of the Giza Plateau in Egypt is one of the Seven Wonders of the World. In fact it is the FIRST of the seven. It is one of the oldest manmade structures in the world, it is one of the largest manmade structures in antiquity, it is one of the most precision and imaginative and labor intensive buildings ever completed. It is also the most mysterious.

Though many historical texts make mention of The Great Pyramid of Giza, it is a fact that none of them accurately recorded its many unusual anomalies, nor reference any first or secondhand knowledge of the original construction project, nor which Pharaoh was buried inside. No records contemporary with The Great Pyramid project have yet been discovered. In fact only one meaningful word was ever discovered inside the huge complex (and it was hidden above a false ceiling). No pictures are sketched in its walls, no symbols or hieroglyphs are in its rooms. This is not common to the other Egyptian Pyramids, many of them have both pictures and hieroglyphs inside. Nor do any of the others have a similar labyrinth of passages and hidden rooms built high up inside; in fact no other pyramid in the ancient world is so mysterious.

Curious, a man builds the biggest tomb in the world then neglects even a humble inscription. Yet we should remember that little is known for sure about this particular Royal Family of Pharaohs. They are remembered in Egyptian history as The Fourth Dynasty of the Old Kingdom Period and The Pyramid Builders, in time replaced by another Dynasty and so on. And with each change in Ruling Dynasties came observable differences to Egypt's religious, civil and burial habits. Sir Flinders Petrie of the Royal British Museum and renowned expert with antiquities in 1905 AD (CE) said of The Great Pyramid, *"the greatest and most accurate structure the world has ever seen"*.

These are just a few of the unanswered questions for which historical scientist still do not agree on a definitive answer. When exactly was it built? Why is it so huge? Why was it built with a mathematical precision that surpasses any others, and do the math equations have deeper meaning? How did they cut and stack so many massive stones? And how were such massive stones transported to the building site? What was the purpose of all the strange passages, empty rooms, tiny Shafts and hidden spaces? And of course, Where is the mummy and the treasure??

Why could no one discover the secret doorway inside? Why did they invert the base as to make it more a star rather than a square, and why orientate it with the stars? Could it have been a planetary beacon or science experiment or even alien? Which pharaoh paid for the enormous labor and materials? Who built a fortress wall around it, then had it removed? Why design the interior of The Great Pyramid so different from all other pyramids in the world, and then actually hide many of those differences before sealing it shut? Is there one historical connection that could unify the mysteries and solve the puzzle??

Of course a good mystery begets more mystery. For instance, claims by notable people of strange feelings while inside, sightings of strange lights overhead and discoveries of strange objects which disappear before they can be documented. Well, if the significance of The Great Pyramid is new to you, just stay with me for the real Interesting Facts! The Great Pyramid is ancient in history, enormous in size, rare in quality and well documented in mystery.

Part Two = INTERESTING FACTS

The Great Pyramid is located in the geographical <u>center</u> of the land surfaces of the world, examine any world map. 31 degrees east of Greenwich is the longest land meridian and 30 degrees north is the longest land parallel on the globe. This spot is said to be the center of gravity of the earth's continents, dividing the total land mass into equal quarters. Curiously the White Pyramid in China and the Sun Pyramid in Mexico, both built afterwards, are nearly <u>parallel</u> on the globe with The Great Pyramid and share construct similarities.

Each <u>side</u> is oriented with the four Cardinal points of the compass with only a 2 foot difference by modern standards. The <u>height</u> of The Great Pyramid times 2pi will exactly <u>equal</u> the perimeter of the pyramid. Its mathematical contrasting between overlapped circles, squares and triangles is well documented. Supposedly if the base of The Great Pyramid is equated with the diameter of the earth, then the radius of the moon can be generated by subtracting the radius of the earth from the height of the pyramid.

The <u>base</u> of this Pyramid covers 13.7 acres of ground, huge even for our time, and the entire base is level to less than 1 inch (2.1cm). The <u>length</u> of each side is 755.8 feet long, each side even to less than 2 inches (4.4cm) and the four <u>sides</u> to less than 8 inches. Even after thousands of years!

All four <u>corners</u> turn at near perfect right angles between 89 & 90 degrees. All four corners rise from the sides at a perfect 51 degree 51 minute angle. Mysteriously the four primary corner stones are <u>sockets</u>, maybe for earthquakes?. No other pyramid in the world has ball and socket corner foundations.

The original <u>height</u> would have been 481 feet high, currently it is 455 with the cap missing, that is more than 35 stories high. It was the world's largest and tallest building until modern times with 201 levels of stepped tiers! The whole pyramid was then <u>covered</u> with smooth granite, 1 foot thick slabs that interlocked.

Many of the foundation stones weigh 15 tons each, some of the Chamber stones weigh 50 tons and the average size stone used weighs in at 2.5 tons or 5000 lb. As many as 2 million cut stones were used to build The Great Pyramid! Mortar was not used yet a sheet of paper cannot be slid between the set stones. It has an estimated volume of 90,000,000 cubic feet and an estimated weight of 6.5 million tons. It is the first giant pyramid ever built. WOW!

Inside Chamber walls are expertly squared. Passageways and Air Shafts are set at corresponding slopes into the level construction. The primary bisections of the internal labyrinth are set in triangular uniformity. Some areas were carefully hidden while others were not. It has several door blocks that expertly raised, lowered or swiveled to open and close passages. The entire Great Pyramid is built of cut stones, not walls filled in with dirt as many later pyramids were! Many more Interesting facts are mentioned throughout the next Sections.

Explore The Great Pyramid community for yourself and see where I obtained some of the great *source material: Dr. Zahi Hawass homepage www.DrHawass.com ; Prof. Rudolf Gantenbrink of the Upuaut Project website www.cheops.org ; Guardian's Egypt website www.guardians.net ; Jenny Hill website www.ancientegyptonline.co.uk ; Iain Hawkins website www.akhet.co.uk ; also Tim Stouse's website www.timstouse.com/egypt ; Dr. John DeSalvo's website www.gizapyramid.com ; and Anthony Sakovich's www.gizabuildingproject.com ; Greg Reeder website www.egyptology.com these each have (2010) great Pictures, Links, and Books about The Great Pyramid of Giza that will expand your perspective and understanding. The Seven Year Famine connection to The Great Pyramid Mystery proposed and proved in this book had not been seriously discussed and researched until now, until here.

Dr. Hawass is the legendary member of Egypt's Supreme Council of Antiquities. Council associates have personally researched and discovered numerous artifacts throughout Egypt and have been an intellectual voice when interpreting the past. Most familiar names in Egyptology have conclusively determined The Great Pyramid was built by Egyptian peasants and craftsmen not by slaves, over a period of ten to fifteen years. I agree with them and believe it is entirely likely the primary superstructure was built in seven years with the entire pyramid completed after another seven years. *Particularly interesting is the Cemetery of the Giza Builders discovered in 1990 by Dr. Zahi Hawass and Dr. Mark Lehner on the Plateau's Southside. One of the Craftsman family tombs is decorated with scenes of <u>grain</u> grinding, bread and beer making. Oh, and an interesting epitaph, "I WORKED ON THE PYRAMID".

Because most professional and amateur Egyptologist are already familiar with the background fact and theory of The Great Pyramid of Giza, we will simply solve the mystery in Part Three of this Chapter. Considering first its connection to the historical story and then unfolding the verified primary facts one by one till no doubt remains. Of course some of you will be able to expound the details. Facts and theories are clearly noted and the facts are not selective to mislead. I am not the expert but have tried to format the scholarly information for easy comprehension. Throughout are <u>underlined words</u> for quick reference; also * marks brief yet interesting historical comments.

<u>There are three questions you must answer for yourself as you study the evidence</u>
<u>ONE</u>, Can you agree the chambers inside The Great Pyramid were likely constructed first as a single structure, with the pyramid built around and over? (see sections L & M)

<u>TWO</u>, Can you agree the Shafts likely served a practical purpose rather than a religious, possibly as loading shafts? (see sections H & I)

<u>THREE</u>, Can you agree the following historical Text insinuates that corn was gathered separately into one place under the Hand of Pharaoh? (see section A)

If we end up agreeing on these three answers, than the so called Great Famine connection to The Great Pyramid will soon become self evident. Now, Let us begin; let us see why this Pharaoh built this Pyramid so different?

Part Three = THE DUAL USE THEORY

This book proposes The Great Pyramid was designed with a Dual Use purpose and the intent of that Dual Use was a Silo and Tomb Design. The Great Pyramid of Giza was to appear both outwardly and inwardly as a proper tomb for a Royal Pharaoh of Egypt. This proper tomb was obviously planned into the original design, but a plan inside a plan is apparent. The original design incorporating another purpose with the final 'tomb' parts of construction literally covering over 'other' seemingly useless parts that were constructed first. The other purpose would have a limited time period to function and must have been worth the extra effort. What was this other purpose?

Simple and practical and recorded in ancient text; The firm conviction of a powerful Pharaoh that a severe famine was coming upon Egypt and the surrounding counties in only several years time and would last for several years, according to dreams and signs of forewarning. Pharaoh believed this famine would come and took appropriate measures. The <u>Dual Use Theory</u> says The Great Pyramid of Giza was designed for two separate purposes. A <u>Silo and Tomb Design</u> says it was first as a Temporary Grain Silo and second as a Permanent Tomb. The first would make him the richest man in the world and the second would be his world famous memorial. This Egyptian Pharaoh was a builder and a businessman. Everything we know of Sneferu, Khufu and Khafre reveals intelligent and industrious leaders of an intelligent and industrial people. See the following Sections A through Q.

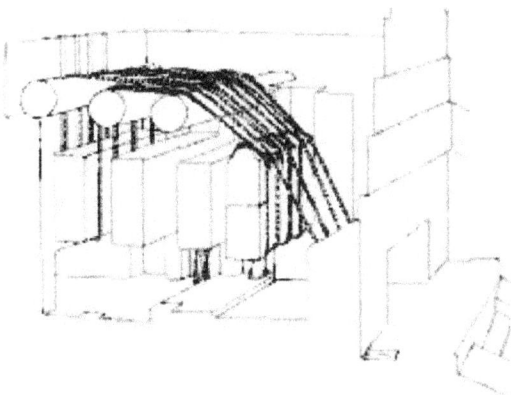

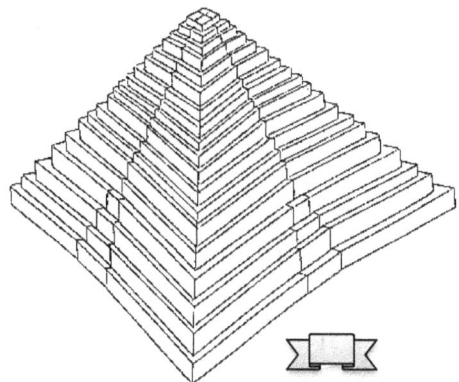

Original and New Entrance into The Great Pyramid

A) ANCIENT TEXT: WHY was The Great Pyramid built?

There is an Ancient Text written by a man born and raised in Egypt, he was educated in Pharaoh's Court and privy to Royal Libraries and Historians. Moses recorded in his first book, <u>Genesis</u>, the story of the seven year famine that plagued all Egypt and the whole region. More significantly, he records that Pharaoh knew at least seven years in advance that the famine would come. This historical text claims to have been written less than 450 years after this great famine event. If the average Pharaoh ruled 30 years then we could estimate about 15 Pharaohs later. *Many of Moses' historical accounts have been proven correct and none have been proven plainly incorrect. He records that Pharaoh, King of Egypt was warned in two separate dreams that seven years of plenty would be followed by seven years of severe famine. He also records Pharaoh believed this completely and made personal preparations for grain collection and storage. The <u>story</u> of the Great Famine is historical from multiple sources, howbeit Genesis is the most detailed and compelling description. Consider the connection to The Great Pyramid of Giza with its loading shafts and tower features that we will discuss in turn.

He recorded in the Ancient Text: *"Behold, there come seven years of great plenty throughout all the land of Egypt: And there shall arise after them seven years of famine; and all the plenty shall be forgotten in the land of Egypt; and the famine shall consume the land; and the plenty shall not be known in the land by reason of that famine following; for it shall be very grievous."* Genesis 41

It continues, *"Let Pharaoh do this, and let him appoint officers over the land, and take up the fifth part of the land of Egypt in the seven plenteous years. And let them gather all the food of those good years that come, and lay up corn under the hand of Pharaoh, and let them keep food in the cities. And that food shall be for store to the land against the seven years of famine, which shall be in the land of Egypt; that the land perish not through*

17

the famine. And the thing was good in the eyes of Pharaoh, and in the eyes of all his servants."   *Notice this, *"lay up corn under the hand of Pharaoh," "and" "let them keep food in the cities."* Clearly there were two plans for storage, corn <u>under the hand of Pharaoh</u> in one place, and food in <u>each of the cities</u>.

This is supported later in the text: *"And he gathered up all the food of the seven years, which were in the land of Egypt, and laid up the food in the cities: the food of the field, which was round about every city, laid he up in the same. And Joseph gathered corn as the sand of the sea, very much, until he left numbering; for it was without number."* Again we see the purposeful separation, two plans for storage, *"food in the cities," "And" "corn as the sand of the sea, very much."*   Remember Pharaoh was <u>forewarned</u> and <u>prepared two plans</u>, one was to lay up corn under his hand, apart from the food in the cities. This is verified again in the story.

He also recorded in the Ancient Text: *"He hath made me a father to pharaoh."* This statement is made by Joseph the <u>second year</u> into the great famine.   It suggests to me that the strong Pharaoh of the forewarning dreams nine years before had died and the son now ruled. So if Pharaoh the father died before his Great Pyramid project was completed, say as construction was between the Middle and Upper Chambers, it would mean all work stopped for at least forty days of mourning while his body was being embalmed. The project would have been disrupted and fallen behind schedule.   This would explain the Upper Chamber being lowered, the northern Shafts bent to accommodate and the overall construction break (see Section L). This would explain the basic Sneferu-pattern employed to design The Great Pyramid (see Section C). This would also explain a younger Pharaoh Khufu 'the son' finishing his father's project more or less in his father's shadow so that little is known of him; and a younger Pharaohs more personal relationship toward this Joseph. *Pharaoh's Sneferu, Khufu, Khafre and Menkure seem to be the family Dynasty associated with the Giza project. It is reasonable to expect the father was buried quickly after the embalming ceremony in a previously prepared pyramid tomb or maybe in a yet undiscovered room added into The Great Pyramid at the unexpected death. During this second year of famine Joseph's Hebrew brothers and families (shepherds) moved into Egypt.

He recorded in the Ancient Text: *"Buy us and our land for bread, and we and our land will be servants unto Pharaoh: and give us seed, that we may live, and not die, that the land be not desolate. And Joseph bought all the land of Egypt for Pharaoh; for the Egyptians sold every man his field, because the famine prevailed over them: so the land became Pharaoh's. And as for the people, he removed them to cities from one end of the borders of Egypt even to the other end thereof. Only the land of the priests bought he not; for the priests had a portion assigned them of Pharaoh,"* he notates this as the <u>fourth, fifth and sixth years</u> of the famine. So the people eat all the food stored in the cities first, then as the famine persisted past two years the situation became desperate, by the end of the third year money failed and livestock sold, they had come to the seed stored under the hand of Pharaoh. Notice the people came to Pharaoh for a share of his corn! The Text does not mention a pyramid, but The Great Pyramid was built by Egyptians before Pharaoh invited the Hebrews to move into Egypt about the second year of famine. Also many of the Old Kingdom records have been purged of great deeds by the next Middle Kingdom, history being written by the victors and all that.

Recorded in the same historical Text: *"There arose a new Pharaoh in Egypt that knew not Joseph."* The textual insinuation is not just a new person of Pharaoh but a <u>new Dynasty</u> of Pharaohs. Less than one hundred years after Joseph's death a new Dynasty of Pharaohs did not honor his memory, but eventually enslaved it as the Hebrews refused to fully assimilate into Egyptian society. Egyptologist agree that only a couple generations after The Great Pyramid was built the Fourth Dynasty ended, after another hundred years or so the Old Kingdom Period ended in turmoil. Soon a new Dynasty rose to absolute power in Egypt, called The

Middle Kingdom. The new nobility seems to have slightly different ethnic and religious views and likely-disliked the Hebrew problem increasing in the ancestral land of Rameses in Goshen.

The Text records that young Joseph was sold by his Hebrew brothers into slavery. That he grew up in Egypt learning the language and custom. As a young man, his master's wife accused him of attempted rape and he was imprisoned. Later Joseph gained the Egyptian name Zaph'nathpaane'ah and married an Egyptian girl named As'enath, daughter of the Priest of On. It also records Joseph became a Governor in Pharaoh's court and such a loyal servant to this early Royal Dynasty that he was embalmed at his death. Then about a hundred years later the Royal Dynasty was replaced by a different one. We know a couple generations after The Great Pyramid was built that the Giza Plateau was generally neglected and within another hundred years the Old Kingdom Period ended. (I realize we are assuming The Great Pyramid was built after Sneferu's Red Pyramid and before Khafre's Giza Pyramid) Both the Priesthood of the City On which was only six miles from the Giza Plateau, and the given names seem more consistent with Egypt's Old Kingdom Period then its later Middle Kingdom Period or Second Intermediate Period. Also, Pharaoh Khufu is believed to have had a foreign advisor, called the shepherd. With Pharaoh Khufu's name is always found Djedef're thought by many to be ether his brother or son, interesting is the phonetic similarity of Djedef're and Joseph'ra. The 'D' would be silent and the name pronounced similar to Joseph'Godly.

The Great Famine set the stage for an aristocratic priesthood of landlords, an indentured citizenry purchased and a divinely connected Pharaoh; all of which are clearly present in Egypt after the Old Kingdom Period but are not clearly present during. Of course the connection between The Great Pyramid, the Great Famine and the Ancient Text is conjecture on my part from the limited evidence available. Yet it strongly suggests that Pharaoh owned a huge Silo that could be easily accessed by all the people and supervised by only a few.

The Ancient Text is an outside connection. Remember, it was written by a man born and raised in Egypt, educated in Pharaohs Court and privy to Royal Libraries and Historians. It has a good reputation for historical accuracy. It admits a negative bias against the current Pharaohs of Egypt and admits a positive bias for the previous Pharaohs of Egypt, less than 400 years before. It does not mention a pyramid, but does make it clear that a previous Pharaoh set two plans in motion about seven years before the Great Famine. One was to lay up corn under his own hand and the second was to store food in the cities. It mentions ten brothers purchasing corn soon after entering into Egypt from Canaan. It mentions the city of On and a nationalized priesthood. It also makes it clear that by the fifth year of famine the Egyptian people all came to one place to plead and bargain for some of Pharaoh's corn. The details of the famine story recorded in this Ancient Text could be describing the Giza Plateau and The Great Pyramid. Our focus being on the building and the Text focused on the birth of a new nation. (see Ch.2 Biblical Chronology)

OTHER SOURCES include the Egyptian papyrus dating back before 1100 BC called 'The Tale of Two Brothers' now in the British Museum. *It is a story about a married man that has entrusted everything about his place to his younger unmarried brother. One day he sends him to his home to bring some seed corn. The wife tempts him to lay with her but he refuses. She becomes angry and reports to her husband that he tried to rape her. The husband tries to kill him but the younger brother flees; and later becomes a king in Egypt. This is so close to Joseph's story that one had to emerge from the other. It is also a lesson on how sly historians preserved the past in hostile environments. *In the city of El'Kab south of Thebes is a family tomb of a Governor Baba dating back before 1500 BC with this inscription, "*I collected corn as a friend of the harvest god. And when a famine arose, lasting many years, I distributed corn to the city, each year of the famine.*" *The family tomb of Ankhtifi is a boasting autobiography justifying his many good works and distributing food throughout his city during "*the long famine which had been foretold*" is clearly stated.

Famines along the Nile River have been rare.   *The <u>Famine Stela</u> discovered in 1890 by American Egyptologist Charles Wibour was written in hieroglyphics and describes a terrible famine lasting seven years. It references the Third Dynasty of the Old Kingdom Period <u>OKP</u> and gives a mythological story about Pharaoh finally appeasing an angry god to end the famine. Experts agree the Stela was made during the early Ptolemaic Era, about 400 years after Genesis was written. It is significant that Ptolemaic Egyptians placed the Seven Year Famine during the Old Kingdom Period, during the pyramid age and not the Middle Kingdom as many scholars do today.   *Picture inside the front cover, 'Corn Collection' is from west of Thebes inside the family tomb of Menna dating back before 1400 BC. Notice the work is being directed by a seated young man with a nobility cap possibly representing Pharaoh Khufu assisted by an undefined older man in the background representing a foreigner such as Governor Joseph.

        If a Pharaoh was <u>forewarned</u> of a long famine and believed the forewarning and made preparation to store corn under his safe control and for his profit, as the stories clearly state; then it is reasonable to believe he might have used the very building type, materials and laborers already in place. <u>He would make Dual Use of his new pyramid</u>. Also remember how a governor gathered so much corn under Pharaohs hand that it could no longer be numbered; no other place known in Egypt could fit the general requirements along with the general description of the times. Only The Great Pyramid of Giza and its many curious features could be a suspect for the "Hand of Pharaoh" mentioned in the Ancient Text. Now we must consider if it has a Silo and Tomb Design, and could possibly share time frames with the story.

B) TIME LINE: WHEN was The Great Pyramid built?

The Time Period is close enough for serious consideration, if we consider the similarities. One major reason this idea has not floated around much before is because the historical dating of The Great Pyramid, the dating of Pharaoh Khufu, the dating of Joseph and the dating of the Great Famine have fluctuated by hundreds years depending on which book is consulted. Some Egyptologist and Biblical chronologist have dated the same events as much as 500 years apart. And they also disagree about dates among themselves. But, in recent years the dates have been moving closer together. It is nearly impossible to put a precise date on any event about 4000 years ago. The Egyptian dating of The Great Pyramid and the separate Biblical dating of the Great Famine to a nearer time period is significant. I recently purchased a book of historical events which separately dated The Great Pyramid and Joseph within the same century! Currently most history books date the probable building of The Great Pyramid from 2600's to 2000's BC (BCE) near the end of Old Kingdom Period. Most history books also date Joseph from 2000's to 1600's BC (BCE). Genesis was written by Moses about 3500 years ago, between 1600's to 1400's BC (BCE). The bronze door latches in the pyramid's Shaft (see Section H) was dated about 4000 years old.

Current dating process is primarily based on piecing together genealogies of known persons and related objects left behind. A professional judgment call is made about final age and overlap of these persons and objects.

Most Egyptologist do agree The Great Pyramid was built after Sneferu's Red Pyramid in Dashur and before Khafre's Giza Pyramid, so the precise date is relative to the approximation dates assigned to these. They refer to this Time Period as the Third & Fourth Dynasty of the Old Kingdom Period. The evolution of pyramid development during this time period is obvious and the pattern used for The Great Pyramid only fits into this time period. We will discuss this evolutionary pattern in more detail.

If The Great Pyramid's mysterious location, size, functional layout and finishing wealth dates to the Great Famine story about collecting corn under Pharaoh's Hand is the key connection and is verified; then the solid physical evidence will require the fluid dates to conform. In fact, as we will see, all the pieces of The Great Pyramid puzzle will connect into the Great Famine story too easily to be ignored. The Time Period is close enough, possibly unifying these two events. (Ch.2 History of Egypt)

Admittedly the official dates are a problem, but the dating of such ancient events are admittedly unreliable. Professionals have 'preferred dates' for ancient events 4000 years ago that fit into their 'personal time lines' but also keep an open mind. *For instance, many believe Egyptian history begins with the second son of Ham named MizRa'im at Memphis, others believe it begins with Men'es said to be the first Pharaoh. The point is the official dates still fluctuate.

Consider if the time periods are the same, this would mean Khufu and Joseph knew each other personally. That is an amazing thought. If true, it would also mean this shepherd king Joseph could have sold corn for this Pharaoh Khufu from the platform of The Great Pyramid of Giza. That before this Great Pyramid in Egypt the twelve sons of Jacob stood together for the very first time. That two tribes of Israel through Joseph are essentially part Egyptian. Moses' claim, that he carried Joseph's bones out of Egypt during the exodus. (Ch.2 Biblical Chronology)

Consider the fact that very little has been discovered about Pharaoh Khufu/Cheops or Governor Zaph'nathpaane'ah/Joseph, different names in different languages. It was a golden age of Hamitic Kingdoms yet extremely few contemporary records have survived. Old Kingdom Pharaohs may have ruled as a family unit rather than a person, significantly reducing the time period of each Dynasty; or appointed Kings to rule each part of Egypt under Pharaoh's authority as the Persians ruled, causing today's list of ancient Pharaohs to be even longer including wealthy Governors or loyal Brothers also buried in pyramids and mastabas. Consider some historical <u>Lists</u> include Khufu's mysterious son or friend Djedef (Joseph?) and other names as Pharaohs in their own right, and some do not. All the Thutmoses and Amenhoteps; or confusion between a birth name, a chosen name, or titles claimed but not possessed. *The old Kings of England always claimed to be the rightful ruler of France, Scotland and Ireland; even so these places at different times had their own Kings. The Mongolian Genghis Khan claimed to rule most of China and so did the Chinese Jade Emperor. In truth, they both ruled the people of China at the same time in different ways. References to Pharaohs Tcheser, <u>Djoser</u> and Zoser seem to be the same person with the famed <u>Imhotep</u> and most Egyptologist agree with that assumption. *A group of German historians are now proposing that some of the Pharaohs may have ruled at the same time. And so more Egyptologist are now believing early Egyptian Dynasties may overlap each other, all of which would move the <u>Time Period of The Great Pyramid</u> closer to <u>2000 BC (BCE)</u>.

The <u>Turin List</u> of Egypt's Kings was discovered in 1820 at Thebes (Luxor). The papyrus document is in 160 fragments and was written during the New Kingdom Period about the time of Ramesses II. Not all the names line up with other List or monuments. For example <u>Manetho</u> reference Khufu as living or ruling about 63 years but the Turin List him ruling 23 years and then Djedefre 8 years, the Seti List omits Djedefre altogether.

*The English word Egypt was once called Misrayim (Hamitic; of Mizraim) and Hakuptah (Semitic; of Memphis) and Kemet (black country) or Deshret (red country) and Tameri (beloved land).

c) THE PHARAOHS: WHO built The Great Pyramid?

The first notable stone pyramid in Egypt and possible the world is the impressive Step Pyramid of Saqqara outside the ancient capitol of Memphis. It is believed the Step Pyramid was designed by <u>Pharaoh Djoser</u> and his engineer-priest <u>Imhotep</u>. Afterward some lesser known and lesser impressive pyramids were built. These solid pyramid markers usually set over top of underground burial chambers like giant grave stones.

Then comes a sudden improvement in pyramids with <u>Pharaoh Sneferu</u> called Soris. He is rumored by early historians to have been a wise ruler and enjoyed years of extremely good mining and harvest. He is credited with building the impressive Meidum Pyramid, Bent Pyramid and the nearly perfect triangle Red Pyramid. The basic pattern of these three pyramids was the same used for The Great Pyramid, so that we would have to consider that Sneferu or his engineer-priest may have designed The Great Pyramid and even began the project before his death. His pyramids began the <u>Sneferu-Pattern</u> of setting doorways high up into the pyramid structure itself rather than directly into the ground nearby the structure. From the doorway he set a long descending passageway passing down through the pyramids into the foundation below. His pyramids also featured burial chambers just above ground level inside the pyramid structure. *And most important here, we can see the chambers were constructed first with the pyramid erected around and over them. His pyramids were also covered over with a smooth surface of limestone. Inside his Red Pyramid is a unique chamber ceiling that is nearly identical to the Gallery ceiling inside The Great Pyramid which gradually tappers together. It is believed Sneferu married <u>Queen Hetepheres</u> and they had at least four sons, one of whom is Khufu, credited for building The Great Pyramid of Giza.

Khufu's Great Pyramid is far larger and more complicated than anything ever seen before. It incorporates the basic Sneferu-pattern and includes many other 'first' in structural design. So that Sir Flinders Petrie whom spent many years working in Egypt said The Great Pyramid was, *"the greatest and most accurate structure the world had ever seen"*. We will examine many of those features in turn and point out there connection to the historical famine story already mentioned. Most significantly here the Sneferu-Pattern is followed and improved, particularly in building the inside chambers first then constructing the pyramid around and over. If the interior design of The Great Pyramid is considered from that perspective, then the silo space of The Great Pyramid becomes evident beneath the loading Shaft inlets and the chamber floors! (A MISSING LINK) Because The Great Pyramid has been generally viewed like a giant cake built layer upon layer, the Silos have gone unnoticed. The top of both silos converted into a beautiful chamber complete with false floors. *Consider that the ancient Egyptian pyramid builders never constructed a free floating empty chamber high inside a stone structure before or after this pyramid and most likely did not know how, neither had they yet discovered ceiling domes nor archways. They always built the empty chambers first then the pyramid around and over, besides you will see this silo space can be verified.

It is believed Pharaoh Khufu called Suphis I and Cheops was either married or sibling to Princess Henutsen whom son was Khafre. (Cheops is the Greek name for Khufu and Chephren is the Greek name for Khafre) The Great Pyramid of Giza, first of the Seven Wonders of the World, is mysteriously assigned to him without complete certainty. In the past some have speculated if there ever was a Pharaoh Khufu. Nevertheless he is credited with building The Great Pyramid, but it seems more likely Sneferu or his engineer-priest designed and even started this project, Khufu completing it with improvements; under the shadow of his famous father. Finally in 1837 his name was discovered written inside a secret chamber. *Just before this publication his name was discovered a second time on a boat buried just outside his Great Pyramid. Pharaoh Khufu is rumored to have been a hard task master. Likely his race was Hamitic (black) and his family could probably trace direct lineage back to Lower Egypt's founding fathers. He built the greatest pyramid rising 481 feet into the sky but *today nothing else of him survives except one tiny statue only 3 inches tall. At least there is no doubt the actual labor was done by Egyptian Craftsman and peasants. Newly discovered Giza labor camps and cemeteries along with the observable progression in construction techniques and localized artifacts all but confirm it. Hopefully one of these crafter's tombs will contain a first-hand account of The Great Pyramid project!

Between Khufu and Khafre, some believe was Djedefre, also known as Pharaoh Ra'djedef. His name appears in the *Turin List of Pharaohs which was made about the time of Rameses II during the New Kingdom Period, nearly a thousand years after this time period. This List sometimes disagrees with other List (Seti List) on the names and dates of ancient Pharaohs which do not reference Djedef, but it is a valuable source of information. *Both historians Herodotus and Manetho spoke of a mysterious Shepherd King that was guide to Pharaoh Khufu. Djedef're built the Pyramid of Abu Rawash some five miles north of Giza, nearer the land of Goshen and not with Khufu's Great Pyramid or Khafre's Giza Pyramid. Also his Mother is unknown, unrecorded as if he were a foreigner. His relationship to Khufu is still uncertain, even so their names appear together about the Giza Plateau. His pyramid is much smaller and was reopened not so long after his burial. These particulars plus the obvious similarity between jedef and joseph makes me wonder; Governor Djedef're?

Next comes the Pyramid of Khafre, he is thought by some to be Khufu's son or nephew and he is rumored to have been an extremely wealthy King. *Consider the coincidence that Khufu's father is documentedly rumored to have enjoyed great harvest, and Khufu's son to have been extremely wealthy, while Khufu himself built a strange supra-pyramid that resembles a corn silo. Khafre's Pyramid is the big one next to the Great Pyramid and appears taller from a distance but it was actually built on higher ground and rises up 470 feet. This pyramid is aligned directly behind the Sphinx. It has one large burial chamber, complete with a peaked ceiling just above ground level in the pyramid center and consistent with the Sneferu-pattern. (see diagrams) It is believed Pharaoh Khafre called Suphis II and Chephren was married to Meresankh III and Khamerernebty I by whom his son Menkare was born.

Menkare's Pyramid is the third big pyramid on the Giza Plateau and rises up 216 feet. Around these three primary pyramids are many small pyramids and mastabas for royal family and friends. It is believed Pharaoh Menkare married Queen Khamerernebty II and had many children. *A rumored story states he was heartbroken over the premature death of his daughter and had her buried in a gold coffin in the shape of a cow. After Pharaoh Menkare the Giza Plateau is slowly abandoned for the more traditional burial locations and after a time it was even neglected. Pharaohs returned to building solid pyramid markers over an underground burial chamber or no pyramid at all till the practice finally disappeared and the knowledge lost.

These Pharaohs managed the most advanced society of their time. Most of what is known about them comes from studying their monuments, the history text recorded by much later dynasties, and traditional stories passed down by Egyptian priest. All three of these testify The Great Pyramid was completed by Pharaoh Khufu with the assistance of Djedef.

Forth Dynasty Pharaohs (Old Kingdom)

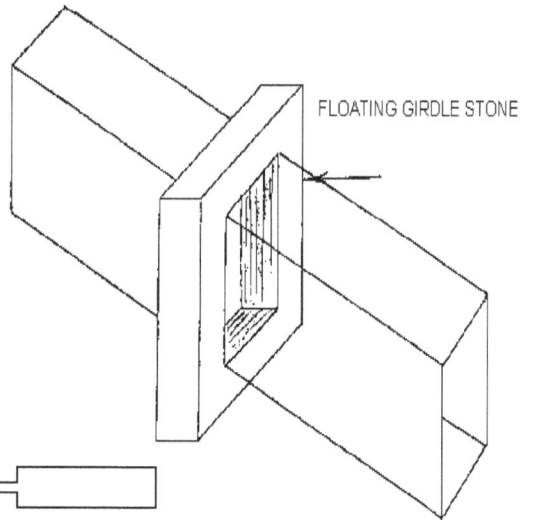

FLOATING GIRDLE STONE

(top) Great Pyramid Corridor & Great Pyramid Shaft (bottom)

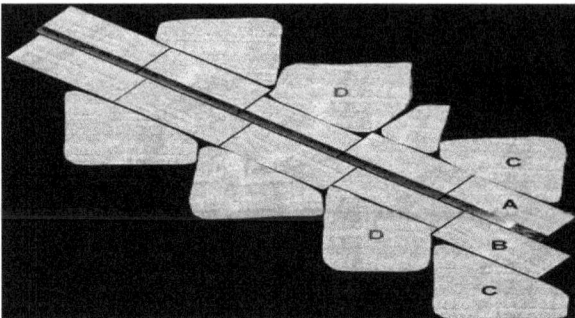

D) THE LOCATION: WHERE was The Great Pyramid built?

The Location of this pyramid is curious. Memphis was the capitol of the two-lands, Upper and Lower Egypt. The Giza Plateau is well north of the capitol and the other burial pyramids. The Great Pyramid was built in what could be considered old Egypt's northern most defensible position, well inside the boarder at a point before the Nile begins to fork apart, next to the village of Cairo. *Today Cairo is a major city of some 29 million people and has stretched right up to the Ghiza Plateau. The Great Pyramid was also the first pyramid built on the Plateau and this far north. Mysteriously the door into the Pyramid does not face Egypt proper but rather away northward. Before the doorway was a great patio or platform with a raised walkway descending pass the Sphinx toward the River Nile.

As mentioned in the Introduction, this mighty Sphinx was built about the same time as The Great Pyramid. It does not watch over a dead Pharaoh but looks toward the Mediterranean Sea and the land of Canaan, as if it were welcoming visitors. The Great Sphinx symbolizing the nation of Egypt, the body of a powerful people at peace with Pharaoh as its head. A modern day child may be tempted to think it was all an ancient amusement park. With all the wear along its body, I suspect many a child has played on it. *A well known story is found written on a stone placard before the Sphinx. A young Thutmose was out hunting when he grew tired and laid down to sleep under the shade of the giant head of the Sphinx. It was mostly buried by the drifting sand. He claimed to have a dream where he was told to dig out and free the Sphinx and he would become Pharaoh of Egypt. When he awoke young Thutmose began the huge task of digging out and repairing the great Sphinx. Afterwards he apparently became Pharaoh Thutmose IV (Menkheperure) and commissioned the placard with his testimony. *In Greek Mythology, the Sphinx guarded the road and would let none pass unless he or she could answer a riddle. It had the head of a woman and the body of a lion and waited. One day Edipus came to pass that way and the Sphinx asked him, *"What walks on four legs in the* *morning, then two legs during midday and in the evening on three legs?"* After only a moment he answered, *"That is simple, a man. As a baby he crawls on all fours then walks tall in youth and after uses a staff in old age."* The Sphinx was suddenly horrified and fell to its death.

Consider The Great Pyramid is located next to the <u>Nile River</u> flowing down from the South of Upper Egypt northward through Lower Egypt into the Mediterranean Sea; and it is located along the two ancient <u>Trade Roads</u> of Canaan and Arabia connecting within Egypt toward Libya westward or Nubia southward. It was perfectly situated for Egyptian farmers and merchants to deliver corn by boat or mule, to be poured down the Load Shafts into the belly of the pyramid silo. Consider that it was perfectly situated for foreign travelers of that time period; *even today the Giza Plateau is Egypt's number one tourist destination. According to the story, by the second full year of the great famine, the wealth of the whole region from Luxor to Lebanon began to pour into Pharaoh's hand by river and by road. People would have come to the great Sphinx and lined up the raised walkway to purchase corn at the platform before the open door of The Great Pyramid. A raised walkway up to the pyramid would have preserved control and order. The platform (loading dock) allowed for the buyer's bags or jars to be quickly taken inside and filled. Consider also that Egyptologist have discovered lots of (travel size) ancient <u>Pottery Jars</u> near the edge of the plateau. By itself it may have just been a busy trading post, or it may just be connected to The Great Pyramid's original purpose, enterprising Egyptians selling simple jars to people that came for corn but did not bring a container.

Interestingly, On is the only city mentioned by name in the Ancient Text regarding an event that affected all of Egypt. The ancient <u>City of On</u> is located only six miles from The Great Pyramid site. This made the Giza Plateau a convenient location for government officials to maintain a civilized house nearby while diverting traffic away from the Capitol City of Memphis. It also made a convenient location for the son-in-law of the

Priest of On to govern Pharaoh's corn supply as the story suggest. At about 2000 BC or so Pharaoh Senusert I built the Obelisk of On which is still standing today; could he have built it in honor of the famine's forewarning? The time period is about right but the Dynasty is not. (see Ch.2 Egyptian History) Egyptologist believe a stone Wall was originally built around the site. This wall along with the obvious fact that The Great Pyramid was built on an elevated plateau made it an impregnable fortress and easily defended by a minimum of soldiers against a powerful army or angry mob.

A large Worker's Camp was recently discovered nearby the plateau, a small 'company town' that appears many of its residence may have worked in rotating shifts. It has now been established that the work camp was for Egyptians working on some of the Giza projects. A large Builders Cemetery was also discovered recently and quite by accident. *The story goes something like this: A western tourist visiting The Great Pyramid had fallen off her wondering camel and broke an arm. The Egyptian boy helping her up investigated what in the sand was so hard as to injure the poor lady and uncovered a stone step. The two pushed more sand away and discovered a second then third step leading downward into the desert. He ran to tell the ever present Dr. Hawass and Dr. Lehner who realized immediately they may have accidentally found the cemetery entrance they had been searching for. Thanking the boy and the lady, began digging out the steps that proceeded down into a massive underground cemetery dating back to the pyramids themselves. They are still proceeding slowly, *but a curious note is one Tomb is elaborately decorated with scenes of grain grinding, bread and beer making, though Giza is not a farming town.

The location of The Great Pyramid of Giza in Egypt on the African continent has been discussed for many reasons. It is considered by many to be the center of the world and many others believe it to be a place of mystical power. *Even General Napoleon Bonaparte confided to his aide de comp to having a 'disturbing experience' as he stood alone inside the Kings Chamber of The Great Pyramid. Though Napoleon never revealed what his disturbing experience was, he did say years later when asked, "No, what's the use. You'd never believe me."   Still many believe it is located in perfect alignment with the stars, and that it may harbor a lost technology.   Some believe alien peoples will return to this location someday because they recognize it, maybe even helped humans build it long ago.   It has been suggested that the Prophet Job of both the Bible and the Koran may have built The Great Pyramid, because he speaks with God about placing a Cap Stone on a great building.   Some others believe it was built during the Antediluvian Age by Enoch himself as a monument unto God. You can find interesting books proposing all these ideas.

I learn long ago that nothing is impossible, but as we proceed, you will discover The Great Pyramid of Giza to be located at the crossroads of Divine Providence and human social evolution, when an emerging Egypt showed the world that anything is truly possible. People came and saw with their own eyes that man had moved a mountain and defeated a natural disaster.

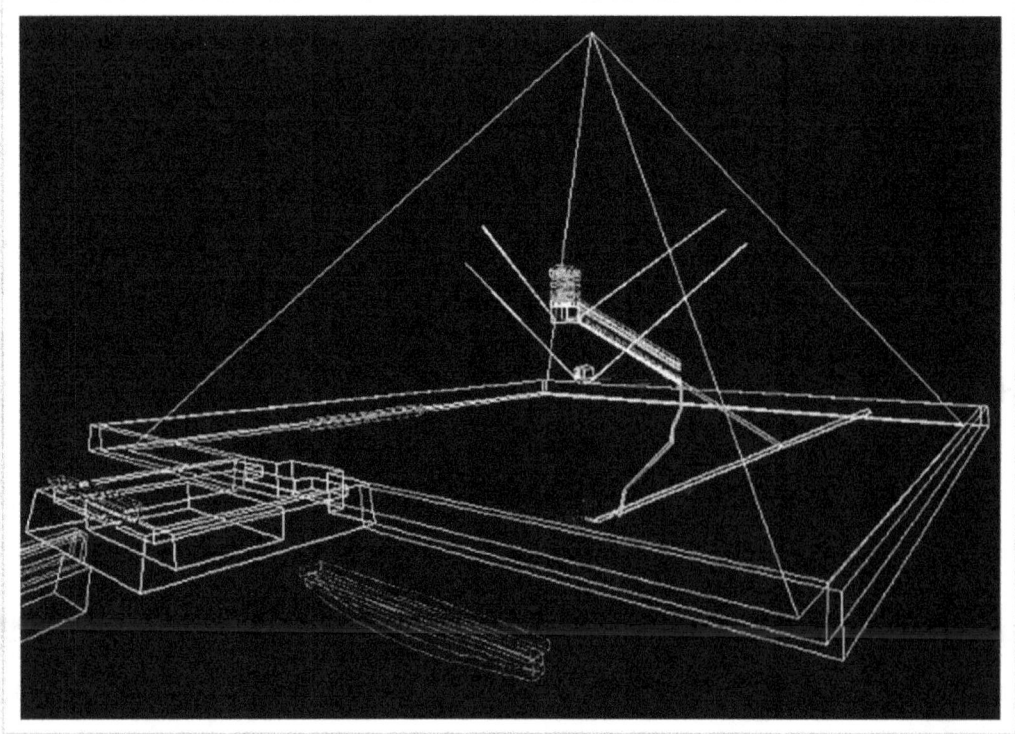

Description of the Exterior and Interior layout of The Great Pyramid of Giza and Structural Details further connecting it to the Seven Year Famine are in the next Sections

Old Silo in Cleveland Ohio using same Tower and Ramp layout as The Great Pyramid

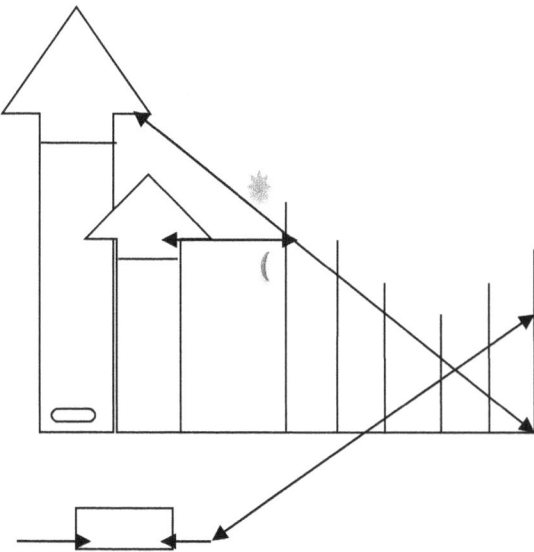

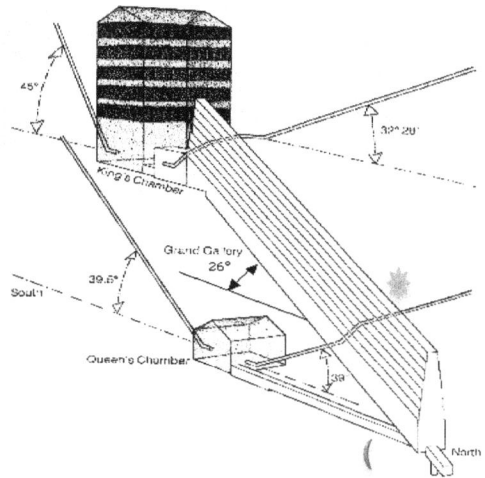

mastaba shape built first

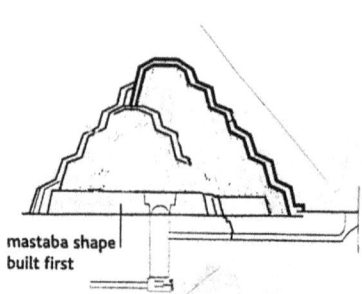

Step Pyramid *Pharaoh Djoser*

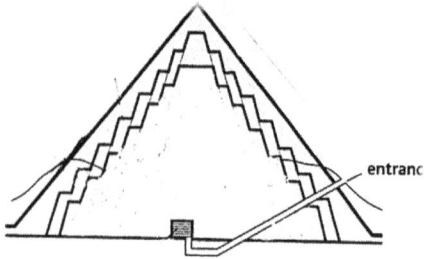

entrance

Meidum Pyramid

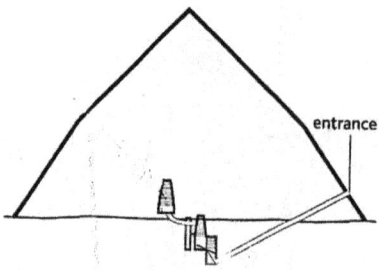

entrance

Bent Pyramid

entrance

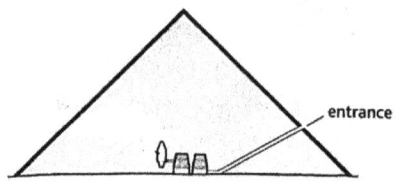

Red Pyramid *Pharaoh Sneferu*

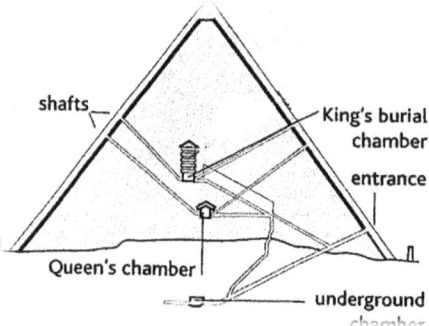

shafts

King's burial chamber

entrance

Queen's chamber

underground chamber

The Great Pyramid of Giza *1st Pharaoh Khufu*

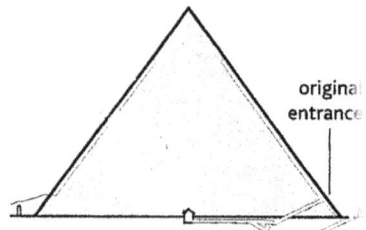

original entrance

Khafre Pyramid of Giza *2nd*

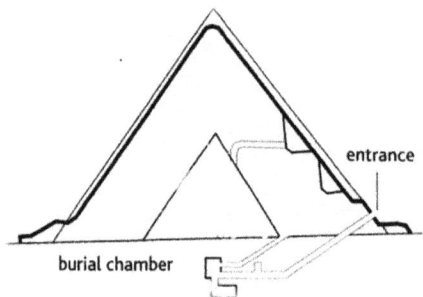

entrance

burial chamber

Menkaure Pyramid of Giza *3rd*

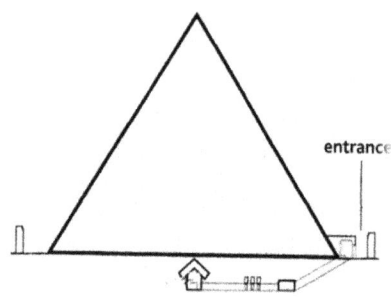

entrance

Unas Pyramid

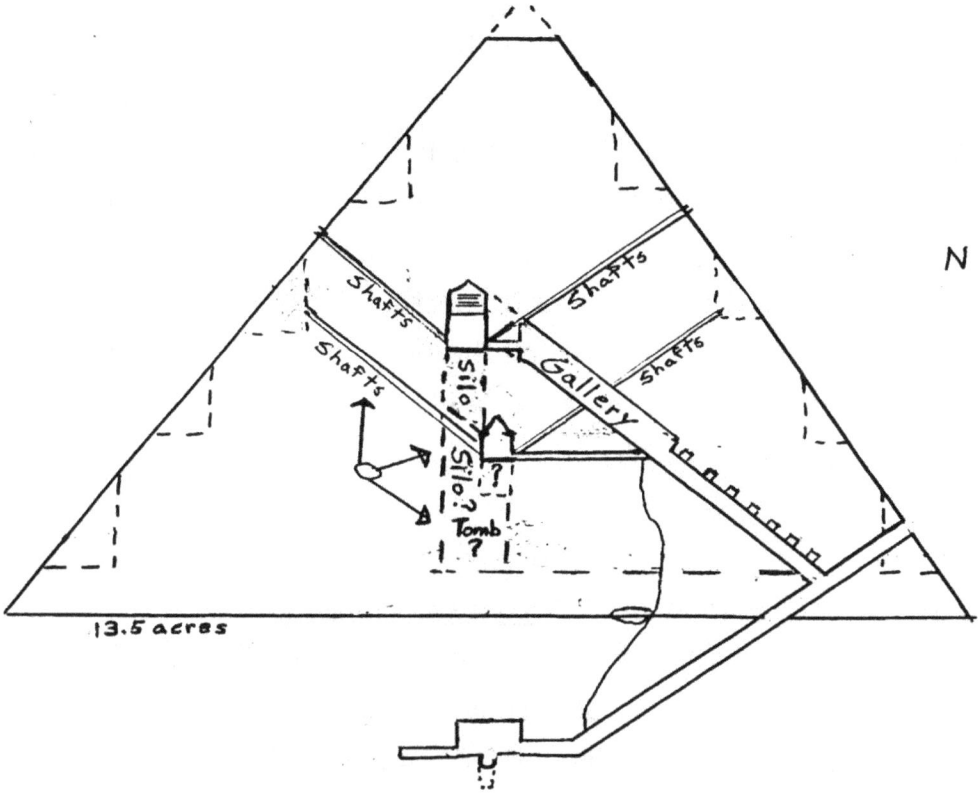

Shafts

Shafts

Shafts

Shafts

Gallery

Silo

Silo ?
?

Tomb
?

N

13.5 acres

E) THE EXTERIOR:

The Exterior of The Great Pyramid is clearly Egyptian and reflects the height of knowledge and ability of the pyramid age. For instance, there are no arches nor domes nor modern math theorems, nether is there any star-gate technology; but there is a lot of precise mathematic and engineering principles. *On one side of the coin, it fits perfectly into the chain of progressive pyramid development during its time. On the other side of the same coin, it is also a giant leap forward in advanced thinking for its time. The Great Pyramid was mysteriously constructed with a higher standard of workmanship and precision then all the other neighboring pyramids, even so it was the first pyramid on the Giza Plateau. This may suggest a higher standard of supervision which in turn may suggest a higher purpose, just a thought.

Only The Great Pyramid base is concave along each side, all others are square. It is bowed in nearly 3 feet at the center of each side nearly making it an eight sided star. *So uniformly that it is hard to notice from the ground, in fact it was not really noticed until airplanes began flying over it. British Air Force Pilot P. Groves took the first picture in 1940 revealing the base was bowed inward. This slight yet purposeful concave sides and the gradual steepness of this tallest of all Egyptian pyramids may suggest that primitive engineers were concerned about unknown factors, such as counter weight distribution and humidity as the silo center was filled. The base covers 13 ½ acres and is perfectly level to less than 1 inch. This is true after 4000 years of mother nature. Each side is 755.8 feet along and equal to 1.75 of an inch. Then it rises up at perfect angles to a Cap Stone peak of 480.96 feet. These facts alone are staggering but wait to we get inside. Remember the world had never seen anything this monumental.

The whole Great Pyramid was then covered over with large granite slabs that were interlocked extremely tight. These slabs were polished smooth and as much as 2 feet thick.

*The Greek historian Herodotus of Halicanasses in 440 BC wrote that the Pyramid shined in the light of highly polished stone. This Greek Historian spent a lot of time with Egyptian priest near Giza and attempted to preserve their traditional lore in writing. It must have been a breathtaking view. Today most of the granite exterior is missing yet its sheer size and summitry is still breathtaking. *An earthquake in the 1300's AD cracked the granite casings and bit by bit pieces fell to the ground and the valuable slabs carried away though a few remain.

Mysteriously the top Cap Stone is missing and has been missing as far back as any historian records. Even Herodotus notates its absence. A Cap Stone is a large single block of stone shaped as a pyramid with pictograms and fitted onto the very top.   *Some believe this strange pyramid never had a Cap Stone but local legend says the original Cap Stone was gold plated and reflected the sun for 100 miles, therefore removed after the fall of the Old Kingdom Dynasty. Finally two small square holes were discovered high up on the pyramid, these turned out to be tiny Shaft Outlets that proceed down through the pyramid structure at a 38 to 40 degree angle. In the 1800's researchers/treasure hunters blasted down into one of the tiny shafts until they realized it continued all the way to the pyramids center.

The Exterior is simply beautiful. A great patio platform was once in front of the Pyramid's large Doorway which is some 55 feet above ground level in the North side and about 24 feet left of center. The doorway has double peaked lentils and was found hidden behind an outer layer of limestone blocks. So the doorway was sealed and expertly hidden. A great wall was once around the perimeter and a raised walkway descended from The Great Pyramid's doorway and patio proceeding northwest ward, away from Egypt proper, down toward the mighty Sphinx and the Nile River. Again the Construction is exceptionally pre-planned, pre-engineered and parts of it are even pre-fabricated. It is also the beginning of an entire Giza Plateau project which can be marveled at from space and discussed in detail by modern professionals.

Around the base of The Great Pyramid are at least seven large subterranean rooms, these pit-rooms are not accessed by any passageway but were sealed directly above. Then the base of the pyramid's exterior layer of smooth granite covered any trace of their existence. *In 1954 AD five of them were discovered to be empty but in the next two archaeologists discovered full size wooden Boats, called a solar ship untouched for 4000 years. The boat was perfectly preserved and hidden, it exposed a greater level of skill than was previously understood. It was carefully removed and now on display in a Cairo museum. (see Photos) The boat, 142 feet long, is large enough to have carried smaller stone blocks and a cargo room sufficient for transporting corn. The odd fact that some of these pit-rooms were built then sealed empty and hidden hints again at the Dual Use intentions.

Along one side of The Great Pyramid are three or more Queens Pyramids that are clearly associated. They are small and mostly in ruin but there is one extremely important fact to point out, *one of these seemingly belongs to Queen Hetepheres, Pharaoh Sneferu wife. We know this because in 1925 AD archaeologist found a shaft beside it filled with her possessions including her mummified organs which would have been removed from her body before burial. The burial chamber beneath her pyramid had been rioted long ago. Most Queens are buried nearby their Royal husbands and she chose to be buried next to The Great Pyramid in Giza rather than the Red Pyramid in Dashur where many think Sneferu must have been buried! Maybe he did start this project after all?. Another of these Queens Pyramids belonged to Princess Henutsen, sister or wife to Khufu.

At first it would have been a tower, which soon resembled a step pyramid. If the center chamber/silo tower with the attached gallery/ramp was built first as the Sneferu-pattern dictates with the solid pyramid structure built up around and over it, then a half built step pyramid was all that was needed to begin loading the hollow Chamber/Silo complex. In fact the lower Shafts end about 25 feet short of the exterior as if they were being used while it was a step pyramid. (see diagrams) Also the first six feet of each Shaft is a level part of the chamber walls supporting a free standing tower theory. The whole pyramid's full size and volume would have been relative; the only concerns being inside atmosphere and the Pharaoh's ego. Because of the tiny pre-fabricated shafts, construction could continue at the same time corn was being collected and properly stored. After the famine had passed, the top of each silo converted into chambers and another layer of exterior stones to sharpen the pyramid shape. The quality of the smooth granite exterior signify a sudden increase in wealth for this Pharaoh far beyond that of his forefathers which used easier limestone.

The proximity and size of the next two pyramids clearly reflect pride in The Great Pyramid rather than shame. Yet they did not include tiny Shafts, a grand Gallery or any other anomaly differing from the traditional tombs, all of this pointing again to a Dual Use purpose for this Great Pyramid. Many laborers at the time had to be aware of the unique interior features of The Great Pyramid but did not try to copy them in the next pyramid. (The Great Famine had passed and now they seemed satisfied to only emulate the exterior size and proximity) If the unique Interior was primarily religious in design, then the following Giza Pharaohs would have been identifying with the unique religious change but not including it in their own burial rites. No religious symbols, patterns or incantations have been discovered inside or out.

This leaves two natural conclusions, the uniqueness had a more practical purpose; and the decorated burial chamber has not yet been opened.

F) THE INTERIOR:

The Interior's Ascending Corridor and Descending Passageway are both angled at a 26 degree slope through the pyramid. The careful pre-planning, primitive yet particular engineering, mathematical awareness, designer tools and logistical understanding are all evident throughout The Great Pyramid built more than 4000 years ago. *A person may enter this pyramid's front Doorway which is 55 feet above ground level and 24 feet east of center on the north side. The actual stone door is missing, but is reported to have swiveled open and closed in perfect balance. Our person would begin descending the Passageway with no idea that if they could walk directly forward through the stone blocks they would run into the Ascending Corridor. As the person descended 60 feet down the Passageway they will see a nice wide opening in the ceiling which is the intersection into the Ascending Corridor, if they continue down the Passageway for nearly 300 feet they will pass from the pyramid structure into the bedrock underground. That person will then pass another opening in the ceiling, much rougher and smaller, which is the intersection into the bottom side of the so called escape Tunnel. About 20 feet up the narrow Tunnel is an open grotto space. The descending passageway finally levels out for 29 feet and the person enters into the Basement Chamber; the passageway continues on the other side of the Basement Chamber for another 53 feet to an apparent dead end.

If our person returns to the first intersection and proceeds upward into the first Ascending Corridor ever discovered in a pyramid, they will be stopped by a series of 3 seven ton granite blocks that had been lowered down across the Corridor sealing the way. Today the person must use a roughly hewn tunnel around them that was dug in 825 AD by a Caliph explorer. Cutting a rough tunnel through the limestone blocks deep inside the pyramid was far easier than cutting through the 3 huge blocks of granite. The Ascending Corridor is 129 feet long, at a 26 degree slope and passing through the center of 7 girdle stones to a level portion. The girdle stones are large stones that were hollowed through the center and act as bridge pylons. Here the level potion intersects with a side hallway deep inside the pyramid. Stepping around a small hole which is the topside of the escape Tunnel, our person would proceed along the side hallway nearly 150 feet through the pyramid into the remarkable Queens Chamber (Middle Chamber) with smooth polished walls and small dual Shafts proceeding out from opposite sides of the Chamber. The ceiling is peaked.

Returning back to the Ascending Corridor, the person will proceed upward into the Gallery portion of the Corridor which is another 150 feet upward, this is also the first Gallery discovered in a pyramid. The impressive Gallery portion is wider and its ceiling rises in grand fashion more than 25 feet high before finally tapering together. The person will finally reach the top step of the Gallery and see a short hallway and antechamber that leads into the Kings Chamber (Upper Chamber). The antechamber was used to seal off the short hallway from the Kings Chamber with a large stone that was designed to be raised or lowered. Here the person would be standing in the approximant center of The Great Pyramid!

The beautiful Kings Chamber also has smooth polished walls and small dual Shafts proceeding out from opposite sides. The ceiling is flat and consist of some of the heaviest inside stones. Directly above is the matching Relieving Chamber which was completely hidden by the false ceiling of the Kings Chamber. It was divided in sections and not polished. The top section of the Relieving Chamber has a peaked ceiling like that of the Queens Chamber. As far as anyone knows these are the only open spaces inside The Great Pyramid, but everyone reasons there may still be secret chambers yet undiscovered.

Now we will briefly examine in more detail each of these mysterious spaces inside The Great Pyramid including where the hidden Silos must be located.

G) THE CORN SILOS: WHY this mysterious layout?

Corn cornels and grains have been preserved since the beginning of civilizations. Egypt is no different, underground pits and egg shaped caverns have been discovered in and around most ancient towns. These were usually topped with a small work hut or thrashing floor. Farmers then as farmers now learned how to preserve their products for both out of season consumption and marketing.

First, the shucked cornels must be <u>strained and sifted</u> after shipping and handling before placed into a storage silo. The rubbing of the cornels produces 'fines' which must be sifted out. The occasional bugs and loose dirt are also removed before the cornels are placed into long term storage silos. This cleaning allows the product to breath, air can freely move between the product as room temperature changes in the silo. Fines can be used in flower and fertilizer.

Second, the silo needs to remain <u>cool and dry</u> and not subject to rapid temperature changes. Cooler and drier is better. The cornels will continue to dry ever so slightly while in storage. If the temperature fluctuates rapidly, it will cause the corn to sweat. This moisture from the sweating of so much product will damage it, causing pockets of rotten material and even producing tiny bugs that will begin devour it.

Third, modern <u>farmers</u> will sometimes add a chemical powder that will further discourage the emergence of tiny bugs and moisture. Some even pump dry air into the silo and others mechanically rotate the product to check for detrition. Because of these technologies, modern silos are only lightly insulated. Ancient silos were heavy insulated underground or in deep caverns to prevent temperature changes and an homeopathic powder was likely added to the product.

The Silo-space inside The Great Pyramid is yet undiscovered, it is the Tower-space that likely lies under the floors of the Middle and Upper Chambers. (see diagrams) The Great Pyramid shows every sign of being constructed round about as a step pyramid with the missing sections filled in afterwards; the same way all the pyramids of its era were built. The corn would have been transported to Giza and up to the appropriate level and poured down the Shafts. It is conceivable they could have used a manual auger from the ground up to the Shaft outlet or driven up the stepped levels. The corn would flow down the shaft onto the Chamber floor. (see Section H) The Shafts Inlets emerge into the center of the Chamber near the floor and make an ideal work room for straining the corn and managing the Silo storage beneath.

The Construction Tower that supports the Middle and Upper Chambers was as hollow as the Chambers themselves. It is a perfect above ground Silo with at least 146,200 to 166,200 cubic feet of long term storage space. (see Sections K & L) We know the Tower to be six feet thick because of the initial level Shaft sections on all four inlets before the proper slope upward begins to the exterior. We can also surmise it is walled in smooth granite because of the Chamber walls of smooth granite. Surrounding the Tower Silo is more than 250 feet of solid stone blocks consisting of the precision pyramid itself. The cool, dry temperature inside the temporary Silos would have fluctuated very little. Even today the interior atmosphere remains constant regardless of outside temperature.

Finally, the body of the Great Pharaoh himself would have been carried inside The Great Pyramid to the Upper Chamber and carefully lowered down the now empty Silo Tower to the bottom Royal Tomb along with all his personal possessions. Sealed away more securely than King Tut's Tomb, yet resting in the same relative location as all the other Forth Dynasty Pharaohs were discovered to have been resting inside their respected pyramids. That is near ground level in the approximate center, but here accessed from above rather than below! The Shafts hidden, the Silos covered over, the Pyramid sealed and the Duel Use completed.

H) THE SHAFTS: WHAT are the mysterious shafts?

The so called Air Shafts are referred to here as <u>Load Shafts</u>. There are four of them, two from the Middle Chamber directly opposite each other angle upwards about 40 degrees through the pyramid toward the exterior and two from the Upper Chamber directly opposite each other angle up between 38 and 45 degrees to the exterior. Each Shaft is about 8 x 8 inches square with minor variations. The <u>inlets</u> are located in the approximate center of the chambers on the north and south walls about 18 inches from the floor. The Shafts were <u>prefabricated</u>, then installed piece by piece at the precise angles through The Great Pyramid as each level was built upward. They are an engineering amassment hidden inside an engineering wonder. *No other Pyramid or ancient building in the world has anything like them, and the extra labor and expense had to be great. Mysteriously, for all the extra effort to build them, the Shafts appear to serve no purpose and were even plugged or hidden. This yields merit to the Dual Use design of this one Pyramid.

The Shafts have a slight curve and enter into the Chambers near the floor level. Therefore they were not designed to be <u>Air Shafts</u> or <u>smoke stacks</u>, which would enter near the ceiling. Nor were they designed to be <u>telescopes</u> to the stars, which would not be slightly curved beyond letting light in or out. Nor a new <u>religious escape</u> for the Pharaoh's soul, since there are two Shafts per Chamber. The u-shape trench was cut out of each block, sanded smooth then fitted mostly downward against a smooth bottom block to form a section of Shaft. If liquid was intended to be poured down the shafts, then surly all the u-shape blocks would have been fitted upward. Today the fittings are still extremely tight, meaning they are not just packed around with dirt but the level building blocks were cut to fit around the angled Shaft blocks making them a solid part of the Pyramid structure. The Shafts are representatively the same as the descending passageway from the Pyramids entrance to the Basement chamber.

In fact, as unlikely as it may seem, there is only one practical purpose these Shafts could have served, as grainier <u>Loading Shafts</u>. Consider that they are the proper dimension and angle for a corn silo shaft, 8x8 inches and 40 degrees. Corn would pour down these with ease, especially with a long turning rod in the shaft. Consider these Load Shafts would have to empty out near the floor level in each chamber so corn could be managed into a Silo pit below. A partial floor provided a working ledge for labor to enter at the top of each Silo pit for racking out the shafts, supervising the filling process, opening/closing the shafts seasonally and later filling portable containers from the pits below. *Have you seen the old post depression-era State Silos with work rooms built on top and 8 to 10 inch pipe coming down into them at about a 40 degree angle? A few can still be seen, such as the large one outside Chicago Illinois. Consider if the Middle and Upper Chamber floors are indeed false and each represent work rooms atop a towered storage area below, then these are Load Shafts.

The <u>Placement of the Shafts</u> inside openings were more important than the other end outside as is evidenced by the extra work completed on the two northern shafts that would have intersected with the Gallery. This is commonly agreed. It seems the Upper Chamber may have been set lower than originally designed. The Gallery seems it may have been widened and turned off lower than originally design, according to some Egyptologist, maybe because they had fallen behind schedule or a planning flaw or construction mistake. Whatever the reason may be, the lower north Shaft would now intersect the bottom edge of the Gallery and the upper north Shaft would now intersect the top edge of the Gallery. The engineers choose to leave the shaft <u>inlets</u> as originally planned, even so moving them further westward would have been the easy fix. Instead the shaft's inlet was more important to the purpose of the shaft and the Chamber than the outlet. So they choose instead to put slight bends in the shaft and to slightly tighten the angel of descent, always favoring a product flowing downward, which made the Shaft installation that much more difficult. The position of the inlets remained perfect because they had to empty into the center of the Chamber pits and be tended by laborers, so the Shaft angles were slightly altered, but not so much as to harm their purpose as Load Shafts.

If The Great Pyramid chambers were built layer by layer there would be no reason to bend the north Shafts around the Gallery because the conflict could be resolved while constructing the Gallery and Shafts simultaneously. But if the whole chamber/silo structure and Gallery/ramp had been constructed first, as proposed here and insinuated by the Sneferu-Pattern, then the northern Shaft conflict would have to be resolve with the slight bending we observe as they reached the preexisting Gallery. These Load Shafts were clearly bent from an unmovable chamber center around an unmovable Gallery with a lot of extra effort to maintain proper width and downward flow within. This is just another small example that the Silo and Tomb Design is a viable explanation.

The placement of the inlets was also significant in relation to the chamber's entrance. The Shafts are located on the North and South sides of The Great Pyramid. The Ascending Corridor and entrance to each chamber is also located in the pyramid's North side. These nearly conflict with each other. Placing the Shafts on the East/West sides would have prevented all these construction problems. Only if these were Loading Shafts would the inlets have to enter the approximant center of each chamber from the North/South walls; simply because half the chamber had to be a solid floor for workers to enter and supervise the inlets. The other half of the chamber had to be opened into the storage pit for workers to climb down inside and load sacks and jars to be hauled up to the chamber. Placing the Shafts East/West would mean the near shaft would empty onto the partial floor and the far shaft could not be serviced. To split the opened floor would make the work room far too small or the pit opening far too small. Also, turning the rectangular shaped Chambers North/South would unbalance the overall weight and stability making the pyramid nearly hollow North/South and nearly solid East/West. The entrance into both chambers are to the far left side, East from the Shafts and so the right side could be open downward into the Silo storage. The <u>Shaft placement</u> was more important to them than the Corridor and front Doorway into the pyramid itself. These were set about 24 feet off center eastward so the Load Shafts could be centered and unobstructed. Egyptian engineers obviously designed the interior layout before construction began and did so with obvious intent of purpose. We are ascertaining what their purpose was 4000 years later.

The two <u>lower Shaft</u> inlets into the Queens Chamber (Middle Chamber) were discovered hidden behind granite wall coverings. All that intense labor simply covered up as if it served no purpose or as if it had already served its purpose. The two lower Shafts do not seem to exit the pyramid, they likely exited the smaller step pyramid shape and were used first to fill the smaller, lower Silo. The lower Shafts would have served their purpose and could be covered over both inside and out as construction continued. The two <u>upper Shaft</u> inlets into the Kings Chamber (Upper Chamber) were not hidden and they do exit the pyramid's exterior. They would have been used after the lower Silo was full and continued to be used until the famine had begun. *An explorer in the 1800's mentions knocking a tiny stone plug out of one. Curiously, the lower Shafts have small 'Alice in Wonderland' doors inside. These tiny <u>door-plugs</u> were designed to be opened and closed seasonally. A wooden <u>rod</u> was discovered wedged deep inside the lower northern Shaft. And another wooden <u>pole</u> with a <u>bronze rake</u> end was found inside the same Shaft. *The bronze was assessed to be about 4000 years old. Clearly <u>tools</u> and plugs were being used in the Shafts, suggesting they had a practical function! *In fact the only thing we see historically similar from Solomon's palace to Julies Caesars' are free standing wood or brick pipes for controlled pouring of grain or gravels, running water to and from baths and fountains or duck work channeling forced heat or sound. Four long Shafts purposely centered at the floor level of each Chamber and carefully angle upward and never duplicated in any other building must have had a very specific purpose.

Another strange fact about the Shafts, besides that they exist and are centered and open near the chamber floor and have removable door-plugs and work tools and were covered and were carefully angled, another strange thing is the first 6 feet of all four Shafts are level. After the initial 6 feet from the chamber the Shaft immediately takes on its approximant 40 degree angle. This is additional proof that both Middle and Upper Chambers were constructed first as a single structure before the pyramid itself. If the granite interior is nearly one foot thick and the independent chamber/silo tower walls are five foot thick around, then 6 feet of Shaft is needed to intrude. Primitive engineers would have to insist on these first Shaft segments being level for the solid stability of the tower! One more fact, *University of Zurich was asked to test residue from the Shafts. The 1970s radiocarbon analysis mysteriously revealed organic residue dated inconclusive maybe 3100 to 2850 BC.

Remember if the chambers were constructed first as the Sneferu-Pattern would dictate then the required space is present for corn storage and the mysterious positioning of the Load Shafts suddenly makes sense.

[Current opinions on the Shafts have settled on a Soul Maze with small locked doors blocking the wrong passages as described in an ancient Egyptian burial text of "Book of the Dead". They suppose this one Pharaoh must have designed his tomb with those passages in mind.]

1) THE SHAFTS and UPUAUT PROJECT:

Professor Gantenbrink and associates in conjunction with Egypt's Council of Antiquities made fantastic observations and calculations exploring each of these Shafts with a small robot car. This <u>Upuaut Project</u> used the robot car to photograph and measure each Shaft block from the inside. Very interesting! Also it provided evidence for a fractional math equation that would assign whole numbers to all the primary bisecting points of The Great Pyramid's Interior layout.

The Upuaut Project notates in the lower Northern Shaft out of the Queens Chamber an ancient <u>tool</u>, a wooden rod that extends up through the shaft and around the bend. A bronze hook or rake that was likely attached to a rod was *discovered in this same shaft by Egyptologist Waynman Dixon in 1872, he was the person to discover the lower shaft inlets completely hidden behind the chamber's granite walls. They also notate in the Lower Southern Shaft that blocks 16 and 17 are offset by an <u>unusual shift or settling</u>, interestingly they also notate this spot lies just under the floor level of the King's Chamber far above. And they notate from block 19 all the way up to block 26 of the same shaft, shallow <u>scratches</u> along the inside: *"Since the scratches extend over the block joints, it is obvious that they were made after this shaft sequence was finished. It would appear that something was dragged up through the shaft subsequent to its completion."*

To me, these three observations may be additional proofs to the Chambers extending down further than the current floor level. Notice the only significant shift or settling of a Shaft block joint is directly under the Upper Chamber where the Silo space should be. Here alone the Shaft must not be secured by surrounding stone. Next, that something was poured down the shafts, over and over causing the scratches across the joints such as the loading of lots of corn over several years' time. Then later, maybe sand gravel too, filling in the old Silo as the pyramid was being converted over to a proper royal tomb. Whatever the cause of the scratches, it signifies a practical, material use within the tiny Shaft.

They notate the discovery of little <u>doors or plugs</u> part way down the lower Shafts. These small stones have two holes drilled through with copper or bronze fittings pushed through each hole. The corrosion is said to be normal for nearly 4000 years of age. Curiously stated in their report: *"But the closure stone was apparently mounted with great precision and held in place by grooves or recesses, without using mortar. Thus, we may well assume that the stone is, in some way or another, moveable."*

To me, this observation seems to be additional proof that these were Load Shafts built for the receiving of a substance, if not corn than at least a wishing-well for coin. The door plug with bronze ringlets could be removed by a long pole with a hooked end during harvest season then reinstalled to properly seal the corn from the elements. What else? These little removable plugs would be simple and necessary for the storage of corn; but no use whatsoever for the storage of coin or the sealing of a tomb. If we combine the discovery of the wooden pole and bronze rakes inside, with the primary positioning of the Shafts, we are forced to admit they had a practical but temporary intent. Temporary because all four Shaft outlets were covered by the exterior granite slabs.

Another curious note in the report; they suggest with reason that an undiscovered chamber may exist on the south side of the Kings Chamber.

J) BASEMENT CHAMBERS and SOLOR SHIPS

The interior Basement Chamber is the first we will describe and then move upwards in turn to the more interesting Upper Chambers. This Basement also suggests a Dual Use to The Great Pyramid. This chamber was carved out of the bedrock below the Pyramid before the first level of stone blocks were laid. The Basement Chamber was mysteriously left roughhewn, completely unfinished and empty. Though most Egyptian pyramids have a basement chamber smoothed and prepared as a tomb, this one was left unfinished by comparison as if all the work to build it was not part of the final project. The chamber is of considerable size, 55 feet x 30 feet x 12 feet high with an opposite hallway leading nearly fifty three feet southward to a dead end.

The Basement Chamber is accessed by the Descending Passageway from the large Doorway into the Pyramid. The passageway descends about two hundred fifteen feet at a steady 26 degree downward slope through the Pyramid foundation and continues about one hundred feet into the bedrock below before it levels off for another twenty nine feet, there it enters directly into this underground Basement Chamber. (see diagrams)

Inside the Basement Chamber is a short ramp dividing the chamber between a higher and lower section. About the center of the lower section is a 12 foot deep roundish Pit or hole, some say it was originally as deep as 25 feet. It's about a 5 foot diameter. The pit does not contain trash or fesses or bones of sacrifice victims. It is directly below the pyramid chambers far above. The pit is deep and seemingly unused and without obvious purpose to The Great Pyramid. Also inside the chamber was a heavy rose-granite sarcophagus lid, belonging to a matching sarcophagus box inside the Upper Chamber, and an unexplained shaft size notch cut into one side corner of the Basement wall at floor level. This roughly hewn Basement Chamber has a busy workroom appearance and was otherwise sealed empty.

The opposite hallway that dead ends has been explained as a sudden change of plans to add another basement chamber, or simply tunneled the passageway to far then back tracked to the center point beneath the pyramid for the chamber. Or just as likely be the space where large blocks were quarried to create a hidden basement room. *If such a hidden room extension is present behind an enormous yet false wall block, a shaft size notch would needs' be on the huge block's bottom corner to move it.

The Great Pyramid has at least three small Satellite Pyramids on its northern side, each of these also have a descending passageway into a basement chamber, except these others all have a chamber extension which served as a tomb. Actually most all basement chambers in Egyptian pyramids have a chamber extension room which serves as the tomb. Maybe, a secret chamber extension has not yet been detected here or a perpendicular Shaft once ran up through the basement ceiling and pyramid foundation into the Silo Tower above for draining down the corn. This would explain the two floor levels with short ramp. The opposite hall would then be a staging area for preloaded baskets. This opposite hallway has never been understood. If it were to suddenly angle upward then it would be a southern entrance, but mysteriously it just dead ends.

Shallow rectangular Subterranean Rooms dug along the outside edges of The Great Pyramid were also added. Two of these seven rooms contained a buried artifact, the impressive wooden cargo Boats, called a Solar Ship, possibly owned by the Great Pharaoh himself. (see pictures)

(Door-Plug in Shaft)   (Basement Chamber)

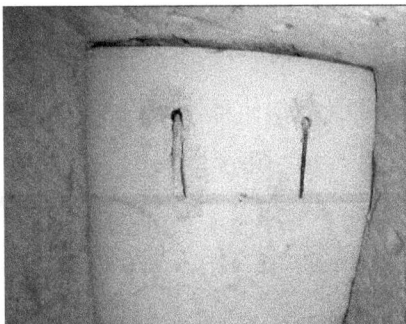

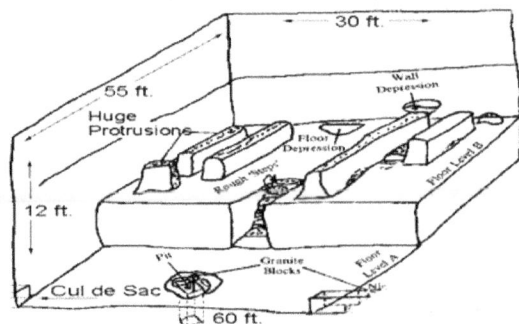

Ancient Ship buried beneath The Great Pyramid edge

Both boats are stamped with <u>Djedef's name</u>, and one has <u>Pharaoh Khufu's</u> name in royal cartouche next to Djedef're. Both names stamped together on the same new boat! The Solar Ships are 142 feet long and were mysteriously buried in 1,224 prefabricated pieces, perfectly preserved and hidden. *One is now in a <u>Cairo Museum</u> and the second is being carefully removed and studied by Professor Sakuji Yoshima. You can plainly see the utilitarian nature of the ship. (shipwright skills too)

These <u>Subterranean Rooms</u> are about 20 feet wide by 50 feet long and completely lined in 1 foot thick granite slabs. These 'seven' large Rooms could also have been used for overflow corn storage. They are not accessed from the inside. They were covered above by 41 huge rock slabs and the bottom of the outer shell of The Great Pyramid. Mysteriously at least five of the outside Subterranean Rooms were sealed completely empty and the outer granite Shell of The Great Pyramid was added after the pyramid had been sealed up tight with deliberate care to conceal these granite lined, empty rooms.(?) *People had been exploring The Great Pyramid for many years before these Subterranean Rooms were first discovered in 1954 AD.

The Basement Chamber inside the pyramid was not finished or decorated or filled with the possessions of a dead Pharaoh. Instead it was dug out with much less care, with a large round Pit in the approximate center of a large work room and left empty. The much nicer Subterranean Rooms outside were also mostly empty. This reflects the Dual Use Theory and suggests the Basement Chamber was being used for some other purpose. It is the only utilitarian, work room type basement under any pyramid.

The Egyptian engineers, knowing Pharaohs mandate to begin collecting the grain oats with the very next harvest did the only logical thing. They dug Subterranean Rooms and Basement Chamber with deep pit into the bedrock foundation even as the first stones for The Great Pyramid were being cut and moved into place above. This was a perfect solution. The Basement was the <u>first stage</u> and would store enough corn poured into the pits and stacked about the chamber to begin the annual collections. The Great Pyramid of Giza seems to have had three silo storage spaces designed into it, each to be ready at a different level of the construction project. The <u>second stage</u> was ready as the center tower reach up to the Middle Chamber Shafts and pit. There continued collection each harvest till the tower reach up to the <u>third stage</u> which was the Upper Chamber Shafts and pit. Continuing till the famine had begun. It would have probably resembled a Step Pyramid by that point, and could have been called a stuffed pyramid :)

The same Ancient Text that describes the Great Famine also describes an older Pharaoh replaced by a younger. Maybe the mature Pharaoh died before this Great Silo & Tomb Pyramid was complete. His body placed inside his Red Pyramid or just as likely he was buried into a secret chamber within The Great Pyramid still under construction. We can only speculate.
And of course the unexplained and rude basement proves nothing of itself, yet if a reasonable explanation can be ascribed to it and the same explanation can be reasonably ascribed to all the other features of the same pyramid then it becomes a legitimate consideration. Let us see.

K) MIDDLE CHAMBER: WHAT is it?

The Middle Chamber, called the Queens Chamber, is located in the approximate center mass of The Great Pyramid. The construction was designed around this chamber, a room about 18 feet x 17 feet x 19 feet high with a peaked ceiling and a large notch designed into the near east wall. The room is beautifully finished, walls to ceiling in a smooth granite stone covering, but otherwise empty. The floor is strangely lacking a granite covering, left in exposed limestone. Above the ceiling is peaked evenly across the center. The Middle Chamber is accessed by nearly 150 feet of hallway branching off the top of the Ascending Corridor which ascends 129 feet at a steady slope upward from its intersection through the ceiling of the Descending Passageway, which descends 60 feet from the front Doorway into the Pyramid. As mentioned in Section F INTERIOR, the Ascending Corridor leading up toward the Middle Chamber was sealed off by 3 seven ton granite blocks.

Mysteriously, there are two small Shaft inlets directly opposite each other on the North and South walls of the Middle Chamber. These inlets were hidden by the Granite finishing stones and only discovered by chance. The Shafts proceed at an upward angle through The Great Pyramid and seem to have exited outside the step pyramid phase before the outer layer stones and granite covering were added to the exterior. Some assume a statue of Khufu or a disc of Ra may have rested in the designed wall notch. Again the Middle Chamber was found beautifully constructed and polish finished, deep in the center of this massive pyramid, empty and undamaged with carefully designed Shafts hidden behind secured granite wall coverings.

This Middle Chamber was the work room on top of the shorter tower which must have extended downward for at least 25 to 125 feet. *18 x 17 x 100 minimum depth would be 30,600 cubic feet of corn storage space. If this chamber was constructed before the pyramid was built up around and over it as the Sneferu-Pattern suggest, then corn was poured into the Shafts from the outside, down into the Chamber and raked down into the <u>Silo</u> storage beneath, part of the floor being left open. Discovered inside one shaft was an <u>ancient pole</u> with a broken off <u>brass tool</u> on the end. This tool was probable used by an Egyptian worker to rake down the corn and seasonally plug the Shafts. Later after the purpose for the corn silo and busy work room was completed, the lower space would have been filled with sand gravel and the large stones for the remainder of the floor would have been added along with the smooth granite interior, hiding the Shafts and making The Great Pyramid ready as a proper Royal Tomb.

The <u>peaked ceiling</u> in the Middle Chamber indicates it is the top of that particular structure. We see in the Relieving Chamber and again in the Pyramid of Khafre and Unas that the peaked ceiling is always the top side of a hollow structure, that or a tapered ceiling created to support the blocks above. Is this chamber simply the top of a middle tower, supporting another upper tower or is it just a hollowed out empty room? The lack of wall art and the presents of tools found inside the hidden Shaft suggest a once practical use for this room rather than a spiritual.

*A near proof to the Silo & Tomb Design was made in 1837 AD by <u>Colonel Howard Vyse</u>. He recorded boring a hole beneath the floor of the Middle Chamber but only finding sand gravel and an old basket before filling it back in. This is an amazing fact because if the <u>Silo & Tomb Design</u> is true then the space under the Middle Chamber floor stones would have been fill with sand gravel from the Shafts along with worn out tools and corn baskets. The current floor level of the Middle and Upper Chambers have not been explored with the consideration that they may be false floors and the proposed pit beneath is still undiscovered. Most likely the room simply extends farther downward, similar to the way the Upper Chamber was discovered to extend farther upward through a false ceiling.

L) UPPER CHAMBER: WHAT is it?

The Upper Chamber, called the <u>Kings Chamber</u>, is located nearly 100 feet above but 'off set' from the Middle Chamber. This <u>off setting</u> is significant, for the lighter weight of the Chamber would have set better directly above. The construction would have been easier to align both Chambers. The Upper Chamber is offset precisely so the relieving support structure behind the front wall of the Upper Chamber could extend up from the relieving support structure behind the rear wall of the Middle Chamber. So if the Upper Chamber were extended downward, it would line up directly behind the Middle Chamber. Essentially the two chambers could be the same structure! This chamber is about 34 feet x 17 feet x 19 feet high with a flat ceiling. The room is completely finished, floor to ceiling in a smooth rose-granite stone covering and includes a large rose-granite <u>sarcophagus</u> which is about 6 feet x 2 feet x 3 feet deep, cut from a single block. Too big to fit through the Chamber entrance, so is presumed to have been placed there as the pyramid was being constructed, it is cracked and missing a lid and a mummy and an inscription.

This beautiful Upper Chamber high inside the pyramid structure at its approximate center circumference. It is accessed from the top of the Ascending Corridor where the grand Gallery section ends into a short level hallway and antechamber. The <u>antechamber</u> is a short hallway specially designed for a suspended stone block to be lowered down to seal entrance into the Upper Chamber. Mysteriously, there are two small <u>Shaft inlets</u> directly opposite each other on the North and South walls of this chamber also. These inlets were not hidden by the granite finishing stones as the Middle Chambers were. The Shafts proceed at an upward angle through The Great Pyramid and both exit to the outside exterior. Again the Upper Chamber was found designed high inside the massive pyramid empty and undamaged except for the Sarcophagus. Even the <u>false ceiling</u> was not realized for some time because of the 9 heavy granite beams that formed the Upper Chamber ceiling. Explorers began to suspect the flat ceiling may be false because the lack of peaking or tapping, they were right.

The nine heavy granite beams, some of which may weigh as much as 50 tons, matched the walls and floor but hid the fact that the chamber actually extended upward. The beautiful heavy granite acted as a primitive steel vault against tomb robbers that could bore through the limestone but would find it nearly impossible to penetrate hard granite.

This Upper Chamber was the work room on top of the larger tower which must have extended downward for 125 to 225 feet. *34 x 17 x 200 minimum depth would be 115,600 cubic feet, plus the 30,600 cubic feet with the Middle Chamber equals 146,200 cubic feet as a very conservative estimate. This size volume would accommodate most of the required space needed under the hand of Pharaoh in the great famine story for corn storage. If this chamber was constructed first as a tower attached to the Middle Chamber before the pyramid was built up around and over it as the Sneferu-Pattern suggest; then corn was poured into the Shafts from the outside down into the chamber and raked down into the Silo storage beneath, part of the floor being left open. Later after the purpose for the Silo was completed, the large stones for the remainder of the floor would have been added along with the remaining smooth rose-granite interior making The Great Pyramid ready as a proper Royal Tomb. Also these Shaft inlets only 18 inches from the floor would have likely been left open because corn collection proceeded here up to the end of the last harvest. Whereas the Middle Chamber silo was filled well before the Upper Chamber silo, so its Shaft inlets were simply covered during the remainder of construction.

This Kings Chamber has been visited by millions of people including many famous persons since it was first opened; but few have suspected they were likely walking atop Pharaoh's still hidden Tomb.

M)   RELIEVING CHAMBER: WHAT is it?

The Relieving Chamber is a hidden area discovered by chance directly on top of the Upper Chamber. The ceiling of the Upper Chamber is false and above is another area called the <u>Relieving Chamber</u> which rises up to a peaked ceiling nearly identical to the peaked ceiling of the Middle Chamber. This <u>secret room or rooms</u>, there are actually 5 squat levels each separated by false ceilings, is believed by some to be for the sole purpose of relieving the weight of the enormous stones above for the Upper Chamber below. This is partly true. But weight above the Middle Chamber is greater, because the Chambers are offset, yet an additional relieving chamber is not above it. The peaked ceiling of the Relieving Chamber strongly suggest it may have been intended to be the ceiling of the Upper Chamber, but the peaked ceiling was set to high or the Upper Chamber was lowered by a construction flaw or time restraint. [At the very least this chamber's height was adjustable.] This is supported by the fact that the Ascending Gallery also seems to have been turned off at the top end to enter the Upper Chamber at a lower level than originally designed. These seemingly obvious changes left us valuable clues to the construction method and Dual Use of The Great Pyramid.

The Relieving Chamber is not finished with granite interior walls. Visible are the stone support structures that relieve the weight above and balance the <u>peaked ceiling</u>. We can see here what surrounds the Upper and Middle Chambers hidden by their polished granite slab walls.   *The primitive engineering is strong and has been suggested by experts to be a solid weight support for a much larger empty space beneath then the relatively small chamber, I agree.   That the Upper Chamber could be so easily adjusted lower also suggest a much larger space beneath it and the nearly identical Middle Chamber! This area above was simply hidden by the false ceiling of the Upper Chamber and left bare. <u>A hint</u> to both peaked ceilings being erected atop the chamber towers is the apparent fact that peaked ceilings marked the highest point in a chamber structure, as seen in other

Pyramids. <u>Another hint</u> is the apparent fact that the Upper Chamber could have been raised or lowered with ease. The Gallery was slightly enlarged and cut off at the top and caused conflict with the northern Shafts, yet the peaked ceiling at the very top was not adjusted lower because it was already in place. Rather the Upper Chamber room was adjusted to the false ceiling above so the height would be the same as the Middle Chamber, creating an unused empty space; leaving workman scribal and exposed supports. Again, this suggests the floor level beneath was relative because the Relieving Chamber extends downward into the Upper Chamber which likely extend farther downward!

I perceive The Great Pyramid structure was built up around two offset relieving chambers with peaked ceilings which extend farther downward, maybe as far as the ground level. One from atop of the great foundation stones up to the ceiling of the Middle Chamber; Two, attached alongside the other or from the ceiling level of the Middle Chamber up through the Upper Chamber to the top of the Relieving Chamber. This tower was Pharaoh's <u>Corn Silos</u> and they were large enough to be Pharaoh's hand referred to in the Ancient Texts. The work rooms at the top of each Silo were designed to seal off the storage areas below and become the Queen and King Chambers, resembling a proper interior design for a royal pyramid tomb. These two Silos are likely the core of the pyramid structure and were built first on top of the primary foundation as the Sneferu-Pattern dictates. This helped the remaining building rise straight, even, and also reduces the number of stone blocks used.

Another possibility for the Relieving Chambers height is its own dual use. The heaviest stone and granite blocks in the pyramid are within and below the Relieving Chamber level, it may have functioned as a sort of ancient <u>Tower-Crane</u> during the early construction phase until it had completely boxed itself in. The stones above that level are relatively smaller. The heavy granite slabs which weigh as much as 50 tons each and make up the false ceilings inside the Relieving Chamber have small <u>rounded groves</u> cut into their ends which could have supported thick ropes leveraging the weight of heavy stones being raised up and set into place. The Ascending Corridor and Gallery is also strengthened by a floor and ceiling of granite slabs. Acting as a primary Ramp attached to the Relieving Chamber structure that could quickly raise and lower stone blocks into place. If we look at the diagram of known granite slabs used in the primary construction we see the Ascending Corridor and Gallery as a double-decker <u>Ramp</u> up to the five squat levels of the top Relieving Chamber, we see the core structure of The Great Pyramid and realize it was designed as side by side towers.

Inside the Relieving Chamber was found another mystery, one word written in the old <u>hieroglyph language</u> with a pencil similar to that used for placement instructions and scribal markings by workmen, where a stone block should be cut or moved, obviously the writing of original construction workers. *Colonel Howard Vyse discovered the scribal in 1837 AD after blasting open the next level of the Relieving Chamber with dynamite. The word cartouche was a name KHUFU. He is supposed by Egyptologist to be a Pharaoh of the Old Kingdom Period, Forth Dynasty also called Cheops in Greek whose father Pharaoh Sneferu was a great builder and their Family Dynasty would have included the time period and style of The Great Pyramid. Recently a second name has been discerned apart from the scribal markings, the name KHNEM-KHUF. Whether a workman was marking the chamber as Khufu's tomb meaning he was the Pharaoh that built this unique Pyramid, or was celebrating the birth of Khufu meaning his father was the Pharaoh that built it, or just as likely a young boy Khufu climbed up in the Pyramid during construction and wrote his own name.

Other than these hidden workman scribbles, no other meaningful archaic writing or drawing has been discovered inside The Great Pyramid.

N) GRAND GALLERY: WHAT is it?

The Grand Galley begins in the Ascending Corridor at the turnoff to the Middle Chamber and ascends up to the short hallway and antechamber entrance into the Upper Chamber. The Grand Gallery is so called because the ceiling above the stairs extends more than 25 feet upward in a grand fashion, gradually tapering together. The impression is of a great ceremonial hall. This impressive looking Gallery is another first not found in other pyramids. There is a ledge on both sides running over head in the Gallery that may suggest the original stair level planned for this portion of the Ascending Corridor, support for the top deck of the stone ramp or it may have been inside storage space for the huge stones that would later complete the chambers. The Gallery abruptly turns at the top step into a short level hallway. If the Upper Chamber was set higher relative to the peaked ceiling above in the Relieving Chamber area then the Gallery could have flowed directly into the Upper Chamber. As it is the Gallery turns off at the top into the short hallway; and the top side of the Gallery's ceiling that meets the wall above the short hallway was discovered packed in with filler stones. This convinced one explorer that the Upper Chamber ceiling was indeed false.

The north Shaft out of the Middle Chamber and the north Shaft out of the Upper Chamber nearly intersect the edge of the wide Gallery causing both these Shaft paths to be slightly bent. These singularities may or may not reflect a change to the original plan but many Egyptologist think it does. It appears a conflict or disruption of some kind took place here. Because the Gallery seems to have been widened and cut off during construction, because the placement of the Upper Chamber seems to have been lowered. The layout and construction of this pyramid is done so well and purposeful that the original plan for the Gallery section and northern Shafts could not have been in obvious conflict and gone unnoticed. *Remember the Ascending Corridor and Gallery was set 24 feet east of the pyramid center while the chambers were centered. This way the Corridor would pass by each chamber on their north eastern side and not conflict with the centered North Shafts. Maybe the Upper Chamber and Shafts were adjusted because of Time Table restraints or the Gallery slightly changed to accommodate another problem yet unknown. Let me suggest the unexpected death of the elder Pharaoh of the 'dream-warnings' would have caused such an untimely interruption in the construction flow. *Forty days of national mourning was required as he was embalmed, this would have caused work on The Great Pyramid to halt. The back to work mentality and scheduled time table required the third Silo/Upper Chamber had to be lowered. It would also explain why a younger Pharaoh is completing The Great Pyramid.

The essential Gallery must have been already in place before any Shafts were installed, because the <u>North Shafts</u> have to be bent slightly around the <u>Gallery/Ramp</u>. The Shaft inlet positions were centered as primary importance, but they still had to be carefully bent around the Gallery for the simple fact that the Gallery and Chamber tower was already built first! Interestingly both bends favor a product flowing downward. The slight bends begin well before reaching the Gallery's edge which again suggest that the Gallery/Ramp was already built by the time the surrounding pyramid structure with Shaft blocks reached it. This is important. For if the Gallery was built level by level with the pyramid and Shafts then the problem could have been easily resolved! Also, The Upper Chamber decorated in expensive rose-granite was very important but its peaked roof was simply hidden. The peaked ceiling was not adjusted lower because it too had already been built as part of the Silo Tower before adjustments to the Upper Chamber level had to be made! Again, what we see is the position of the Upper Chamber lowered in the Silo <u>Tower</u> with a false ceiling installed. This created a useless space above that we call the Relieving Chamber. The Gallery is simply cut short to enter the new level of the Upper Chamber and the strict construction schedule is maintained. Of course if the <u>time schedule</u> was not an issue, then the as-you-go adjustments for easy corrections would not have happened. They could have backtracked any of these conflicts. Remember we are talking about a pyramid that reflects near perfect precision construction, seems odd to let a small mistake of some kind result in this area being fixed on the run. What I am saying with all these details is that every detail supports a Silo and Tomb Design, the Tower & Ramp came first, the chambers were inserted and the pyramid afterwards.

The need for so much temporary inside Gallery storage of so many stone blocks provides yet another support for the Dual Use intent of The Great Pyramid. First the amount of storage space inside the Gallery between the Middle and Upper Chambers. Most Great Pyramid enthusiast agree this space was likely use for temporary inside storage of stone blocks, but so much temporary storage space and all of it empty could only mean the blocks in storage have all been used. The few blocks slated to seal the Upper Chamber does not reflect the enormous storage space created within the Gallery. On the other hand, if the stone blocks required to complete the partly open chamber floors into the Silos beneath and the fancy Granite wall coverings needed to be safely stored close by, then the Gallery would be a grand solution. After the Great Famine was over and all the corn distributed, the interior could be fully transformed into the proper Tomb design with the blocks in temporary storage. By this time the exterior of the pyramid would have been mostly completed.

Consider the ledge overhead in the Gallery, it is basically level with the topside of the Girdle Stones. Remember the Girdle Stones are large stone blocks hollowed out like a giant square donut and the Ascending Corridor passes through their center. First, the 7 huge Girdle Stones would serve no purpose except as a sort of bridge pylons, supporting the construction Ramp until the pyramid structure reached up to it. They support heavy granite slabs from one to the other laid above and within. This new construction idea provided strong support for the pyramid blocks above the Ascending Corridor, but the same effect could have been accomplished without the new idea by just laying the slabs across from one side wall to the other, if it were built in cake fashion layer by layer. The Girdle Stones meant that the Corridor/Ramp could be built first along with the chamber/tower structure as the Sneferu-Pattern suggest. As a free standing construction ramp, the Girdle Stones were needed to bridge the support for the weight of the huge blocks being pulled up to construct the Tower, as the Ramp and Tower rose up together. Together they form a solid stone Ramp that lead directly up to the Relieving Chamber where the heaviest blocks in the entire pyramid are located. Some of those blocks weigh as much as 50 ton and could not be lifted by any manmade suspension devise. I suspect the Ramp & Silo Tower could have functioned as one unit and formed the core of The Great Pyramid.

Along the ledges of the Gallery are 27 small round peg type holes with corresponding niches which function is still mysterious, but if this was the primary construction Ramp than the holes were likely used for pegs that kept the block from sliding back down as forward motion halted. If we look at the diagram of known 'granite slabs' used in the primary construction we see the Ascending Corridor and Gallery as a double-decked Ramp to the five squat levels of the Relieving Chamber. How ingenious to design a Permanente Ramp to the top of the chamber structure for hauling up the massive limestone blocks during construction, then as the pyramid was built around and over the Ramp. They simply converted it into the Ascending Corridor and Gallery!

O) ESCAPE TUNNEL: WHAT is it there for?

The Escape Tunnel or sometimes called the Well Shaft was mysteriously chiseled through the ceiling near the Basement Chamber and extends partway up through the solid stone of The Great Pyramid emerging through the floor of the side hall that leads into the Middle Chamber. The Tunnel is barely wide enough for one small person to squeeze through, about twenty eight inches square throughout, it is completely roughhewn and seems poor workmanship compared to anything else inside. Partway up the Tunnel opens into a Grotto space where the pyramid blocks meet a limestone up-cropping of the Plateau and a small room size space was left open. Strangely a large granite slab was left inside the Grotto space and someone dug a small hole nearby it.

Some assume this Tunnel was dug as an escape route for workmen after they lowered the 3 huge seven ton granite blocks into place across the lower portion of the Ascending Corridor from the backside. Otherwise it seems another useless feature costing lots of time and effort. The exposed holes at the top and bottom were left rude and the Tunnel was clearly not designed by the Egyptian engineers into the pyramid structure as part of the overall design. The overall design was professionally done with purpose, intent, corresponding angles and a certain pride of workmanship, but this Escape Tunnel is throughout rude. Also the huge block lowered into place to seal off the Upper Chamber was not lowered from behind nor those sealing the pyramid entrance. It seems much more likely that the Escape Tunnel was not even there till after *The Great Pyramid was finally broken into for the first time, nearly 3000 years after it was sealed shut. Most likely the Tunnel was added to the pyramid by treasure hunters between 825 AD and 1637 AD.

Caliph Abdullah Mamoun was an Arab leader of moderate power in 825 AD, he is the first person to break into The Great Pyramid. *He is known to have carefully studied it but could not discover a way inside. He then ordered workmen to begin boring a hole using iron hammers and explosive sticks at the place he suspected the hidden doorway might be. The workmen bored day and night till they suddenly emerged into a dark descending passageway, this they followed back to discover the actual doorway concealed up and to the right of their hole. Then discovering the ascending corridor plugged, they bore a hole around the 3 seven ton granite slabs that plugged their way to the chambers above. The limestone being easier to cut through then solid granite. Local rumor has it that the Caliph found no horde of treasure as he had hoped, but only some small golden objects in an otherwise empty building. Even the sarcophagus was reported empty as we see it today. History does not suggest he or the workmen came into any great wealth or technology. Today tourist enter The Great Pyramid through Caliph Mamoun's entrance, proving conclusively this pyramid was sealed shut till after the year 825 AD.

Another proof that the chambers were mostly empty is the fact that the lid to the huge granite sarcophagus was found lying in the Basement Chamber, it would be extremely unlikely that a hand full of strong men would have drug it out of the Upper Chamber, down the long corridor pass both exits then down the long passageway to be laid in the Basement. Most people accept that the heavy lid was never attached and the coffin never used.
Most likely, either he or local treasure hunters soon after dug the tunnel, so called Escape Tunnel. They walked through the empty halls and chambers and reasonably concluded by the overall layout that if a hidden passageway existed to a secret room, then it was most likely between the Basement Chamber and the Middle Chamber and centered in from the Ascending Corridor. This is an obvious conclusion looking at an interior diagram realized at that time. Oxford Professor John Greaves is the first person to document discovery of this Tunnel in 1637 AD, meaning it could have been dug anytime between 825 and 1637.

The Tunnels location at the top is precisely in a short side hallway that leads into the Middle Chamber but the Tunnel snakes a bit randomly before the bottom appears in the ceiling just before the Basement chamber. It was likely dug downward through the solid stone blocks seeking a hidden passageway that would lead them to the secret treasure chamber, similar to the same way they had hammered and blasted through the pyramid wall to discover a passageway into the other Chambers. If the Tunnel had been dug upward, we would have expected to find the Grotto filled with the gravel from the falling debris. So along the way down they dug by the Grotto and dug around there a bit encouraged by the granite slab, then continued on to the Basement. They did not know the original purpose of this pyramid, so the digging began in the very location I might have picked if I were in their sandals seeking a hidden passageway somewhere below. If they had dug down diagonally they may have been surprised. Poor fellows hammered through solid rock nearly straight down to the Basement, with golden dreams of secret passages but found nothing.

72

P) THE PROJECT: HOW was The Great Pyramid built?

A strict Construction Schedule would have been involved moving so many huge stone blocks if the Dual Use Theory is correct.   *The Greek Herodotus wrote by rumor that The Great Pyramid took 100,000 men more than 30 years to build, but today many Egyptologist have agreed on the more likely time table of about 10,000 men and 15 years to build. Consider if the Middle and Upper Chambers were hollow beneath and the outer layers and pointed cap were not added till after the great famine, then the time table is reduced yet again. Seven years is a reasonable Schedule for the primary step pyramid supra-structure to be built. Another seven years to easily complete the entire masterpiece.

No records have yet survived to describe to us their pyramid construction techniques.   Any record of the actual Great Pyramid Project is still undiscovered. With an estimated 2 million stone blocks and some weighing more than 15 tons, we are only able to speculate how the Egyptian Engineers that designed the original blueprints also proposed the systematic method for constructing their project. We must remember they never lived in our modern world and so did not know what they were missing, to them the world was at its height of new technology and innovative thinking.

*Lets' say they were pulling stone from four different quarry sites. Each quarry had four separate teams, each team responsible for excavating one block per hour for a 12 hour work day. That would be 48 blocks a day per quarry for a total of 192 blocks. In 365 days per year, the four sites would produce 70,080 stone blocks. Seven years of steady labor would produce 490,560 blocks, nearly half a million. Add a few more years, double the number of teams, add a night shift or require 2 blocks per hour, the entire pyramid could have been completed in the fourteen years.

Design, Logistics and Hard Work is how it was done. Likely the Basement Chamber was being dug out by a Mining Team as the quarries were beginning to cut blocks. Each quarry may have operated with separate team assignments. *Some blocks have been discovered to have been signed by labor teams with placement markings. Maybe each Saw Team would have ten persons, six sawed on a single limestone block, two chiseled and two levered, set ropes, marked blocks and so on. One or two of them were Lead Men and the others Laborers learning the trade with a lot of father, sons and cousins teamed. Maybe a general Quarry Team came around and gathered the cut stones from each Saw Team, credited their account and delivered the new stone blocks to the staging area where a line of drivers waited. The Saw Team went to work on another. Maybe the Driver Teams were two or three person husband and wives with quad yokes of personal oxen. The team secured the large block behind their beast or onto a wooden sled and joined the long caravan to Giza and the new pyramid. Smaller blocks may have been delivered to a barge along the Nile River and Barge Teams. Likely the center Tower & Ramp structure was built first along with a couple layers of the great stones to provide a solid foundation and core to build around. Some of the stone blocks came from the plateau itself while others were transported from distant quarries. Likely Egyptian Engineering Teams set plum lines and positioned flags while Supervisors directed incoming blocks in a rotation pattern, and credited the drivers. Likely one side of the pyramid may have had several elongated ramps raised against it as construction rose level by level around the core. Maybe the Driver Team delivered the block up to the edge of the appropriate ramp, then deadheaded back for another load.

Here that Ramp Team would secure the block behind their trained oxen while a guide rope was secured up the center of the ramp and pulled tight by men and levers while two hammered pegs into ramp slots each time the block passed one so it would not lose ground as the team heaved and hoaved upward. Once up the ramp to the platform the block was maneuvered perpendicular to the last block set and beside the spot it belonged. It was untied and smoothed out by a <u>Stone Setting Team</u> that would lever it over with solid oak bars and wedges propped under till the stone block stood on its corner and dropped in place rubbing the near side of its neighbor block. This would make the seam air tight between the two blocks. Most of these seams are still that tight today. Wooden rammers perfected the setting. Likely the other side of the pyramid had scaffolding and a system of counter weight lifters for smaller stones, tools, water and so on. *We know from drawings these Egyptians used such counter weight devices to draw water and measurements, and because the antechamber entrance into the Upper Chamber had been designed to suspend then lower a large stone block into place to seal it shut. Special constructs like these, the swivel Doorway and notched insets were done by a <u>Master Mason Team</u> and Likely the step pyramid shape provided a solid working platform each 25 feet or so of height. Likely the ramps were only useful for yoked beast up to a certain point because the blocks drop to a manageable size above the level of the top chamber. Likely a <u>Mortar Team</u> came by with a wheel cart of wood hammers and small stones to seal up gaps. Mud mortar or brick was not used. Likely more Supervisors inspected each team's placement and performance and credited their accounts. Likely strong-backs of Puller and Pusher <u>Hard Labor Teams</u> rotated about by the hundreds with <u>Oxen Teams</u>. <u>Kitchen Teams</u> prepared food and drink for the labors and of course the <u>Accountants</u>, <u>Medical Teams</u>, <u>Monitors</u>, <u>Runners</u>, <u>Military Security</u>, and so on. *You can see the estimated total of ten thousand people is reasonable. Mostly Egyptians of the Lower Peasant Class with young families tagging along, the skilled Middle Class and possible some military and slave labor.

   <u>Transportation</u> of such heavy items at this early time in civilization is still debated. No historical evidence has been unearthed to suggest they had developed air tight buoys attached beneath a floating barge to increase its weight capacity, nor had the axel wheel been invented for heavy wagons or notched pulleys, nor a weight bearing air device of any kind. I admit they may have created an extremely low wattage battery similar to the Bagdad

Battery, but it could not have done more than provide a dull light in a dark room. *The ancient batteries discovered in Iraq only date back to about 250 BC were clay jars with an inner copper cylinder filled with fresh juices and an iron rod suspendered inside showing corrosive reaction from the natural acid, they could maintain 1 or 2 watts. This just reminds us that our ancestors could be quite ingenious with the tools available to them. Someone suggested the stones could have been cut out as balls and rolled across the desert then shaped into blocks, or tree trunks laid side by side like train tracks across the desert or giant kites lifted them or some other ingenious system that clearly never expanded for hundreds of years.

Most likely barges, sleds and wagons were used for transportation of smaller blocks. The really large blocks were most likely moved by simply cutting granite slabs for a slip-road from the primary quarry site to the pyramid construction site, the larger stone blocks and wooden sleds could be pulled by teams of Egyptian oxen or African elephants with only a couple human handlers over the slip-road of granite slabs occasionally slicked with greasy water. At least the slip-road would go from the quarry to the edge of the Nile River. Here a larger block could be centered onto a barge about five times wider on both sides, about ten times longer fore and aft. The block's weight would evenly submerge the mini barge beneath the water and allow a couple people to stand on the floating stone block and poll down river to the pyramid site. *I remember crossing Spring Lake with childhood friends by standing balanced on a small piece of Styrofoam and sinking almost to our knees before getting buoyancy and carefully polling our way across. These ways would be practical, familiar to them and would not cause unexpected supply chain problems. Moving the larger blocks of 15 tons or so would require very low friction, such as a slip-road. Ironically the three large pyramids were incased about in long granite slabs.

A Single Silo Structure 'tower' was likely erected first. This would have been the only queer innovation and so would have been designed first as the solution to the Pharaoh's specific problem. The traditional pyramid design simply encompassed the primary solution. The Middle and Upper Relieving Chambers both share matching peaked ceilings and are precisely offset from each other so that the Upper Chamber's northern wall would share the same set of blocks as the Middle Chamber's Southern wall. If the two chambers descend downward toward the foundation they would form a single structure consisting of a taller and shorter Silo. Also the Shafts exiting both chambers were each set level for 6 feet outward before their true angle begins, telling us these Chambers have independent walls about 6 feet thick. As we see in section M, the height of the Upper Chamber was adjustable. These facts along with the Sneferu-Pattern of building the chamber before the pyramid point us to consider a single Silo tower structure.

Likely the Silo Tower/Relieving Chamber/Upper Chamber/Middle Chamber in conjunction with the attached Ramp/Ascending Corridor/Gallery was designed to act as a primitive Tower Crane & Ramp till the Construction completely surrounded and surpassed it. The Ramp & Tower was literally buried inside and transformed into Corridor and Chambers. *Similar to the way we build some tall buildings today, with an elevator shaft and stair well first and use them to move building materials up and down. This may explain why the top Reliving Chamber was divided into five squat spaces each separated by four levels of extremely heavy granite slabs and why these weight bearing slabs have rounded notches cut into the ends, each level servicing a different side of the pyramid. This may explain why all the heaviest blocks are part of the center Chambers or below. This may also explain how this small advancement in construction technology disappeared after The Great Pyramid was completed. The Tower-Crane & Ramp was a solid stationary innovation of ordinary conception, with long cords set into the notches above and teams of oxen below. Some of the stone blocks could be pulled up then hosted about and maneuvered with relative ease by a trained crew of men and beast.

There is every reason to believe early civilization utilized domesticated beast of burden to their full potential. They may not have possessed machines of gears and levers, but likely they viewed animals as natural machines and used them as such. Many people lived with their animals and completely understood how to best use them. They are capable of performing a staggering amount of work for their food and a loving scratch behind the ear. Egyptian cattle, African elephants and camels are easily domesticated. These people also possessed tools of wood, bronze metals, natural elements and problem solving skills equal to our own. They only lacked our exposure for a modern imagination of what is truly possible; even today our imagination is limited by its experience and need to evolve. Hopefully this section has painted an adequate picture of how The Great Pyramid may have been built, most of the ideas expressed by experts.

The Scheduled time table for this project required design, approval, logistics and construction of a step pyramid well above the Relieving Chamber level in less than seven years. Consider if the Pharaoh had already laid plans for a Giza Plateau project and simply made alterations to supersize it with the revelation of the Great Famine coming in seven years time. Or the likely possibility that Pharaoh Sneferu himself actually started this pyramid in Giza with his experienced builders and died only a couple years into his newest project. He had recently completed the lovely Red Pyramid at Dashur which has curious pattern similarities found on The Great Pyramid, as if the same people had a hand in both. Khufu seeing fathers project through to completion and improving upon it. The first part of this project had to proceed in relative haste and familiar technical confidence, the second half could proceed at a slower pace. That is exactly what structurally appears to have happened.

Q) THE CONNECTION: COULD it be?

The Dual Use Theory provides a reasonable explanation to this unique pyramid's many mysteries and its many mysteries reasonably explain a Silo & Tomb Design. Remember the three questions you must answer for yourself while studying the evidence.

ONE, Can you agree the chambers inside The Great Pyramid were likely constructed first as a single structure, with the pyramid built around and over? (see Ch.2 Fifth Proposal)

TWO, Can you agree the Shafts likely served a practical purpose rather than religious, possibly as loading shafts? (see Ch.2 Second Proposal)

THREE, Can you agree the historical Text insinuates that corn was gathered separately into one secure place under the hand of Pharaoh? (see Ch.2 Third Proposal)   If we have ended up agreeing on these three answers, than the so called Great Famine Connection to The Great Pyramid is self evident. The only substantial hurdle is the Time Line (see Ch.2 History of Ancient Egypt). Does the story in Genesis and this pyramid converge somewhere in the middle (see Ch.2 Biblical Chronology).

The Great Pyramid of Giza is a marvel. Tall and beautiful, enormous and powerful; grand yet functionary without any signs of fancy artistry. Try to imagine a great Pharaoh organizing hundreds of engineers, masons and labor teams. Imagine the Egyptians building this world wonder before any invention we consider modern or even pre modern when the average city population numbered in the hundreds. Imagine thousands of huge stone blocks as they were cut out and numbered and prepared for transport. Imagine miles of orderly caravans moving across the sand. Imagine teams of men and women measuring, shaping, hoisting, singing songs in unison as they worked. Together laughing and crying and pulling and pushing. Hot Sun rising, Nile River flowing, Desert Sand blowing beyond the Green Reeds! See in your mind's eye as farmers bring a fifth part of the land, corn as the sand of the sea. Imagine this manmade mountain, and Marvel.

CHAPTER TWO   PROOF POSITIVE:

"Answers are often found hiding in plain sight" SSD

Part One = SEVEN PROPOSALS

These seven proposals can be proven with a simple proof positive experiment. Before we discuss it, let us examine the reasoning for each proposal based on the many details outlined in the previous chapter. Or skip ahead to the History of Ancient Egypt Outline or the story Khufu's Gold.

This book proposes The Dual Use Theory as the solution to the mysteries of The Great Pyramid. Second, this book proposes The Silo & Tomb Design as the intent of the dual use. Third, direct connection between The Great Pyramid and the Great Famine so famously recorded in antiquity. Forth, the escape Tunnel was dugout between 825 and 1650 AD (CE). Fifth, the Relieving Chamber and Gallery was the topside of the first Tower-Crane & Ramp used to raise up the heavy stones seen within the chambers. Sixth, the King and Queen Chambers extend downward beneath the current floor levels into a yet hidden space, as the Relieving Chamber does, constructed as a single tower. And Seventh, a Royal Pharaoh is still entombed at the bottom level of the Kings Chamber with his buried treasures, waiting.

First Proposal, The Dual Use Theory is a good explanation to the mysteries of The Great Pyramid, even if one was not yet willing to accept the Silo and Tomb Design. For instance, all the other pyramids in Egypt have a clear purpose as tomb or monument. Even so the larger pyramids may differ in precise angles and interior design, they still reveal a single purpose and progression. The Meidum Pyramid, The Bent Pyramid, the Red Pyramid all have the burial chamber at or about the center base or ground level. Then suddenly comes The Great Pyramid more than twice as big with the so called Burial Chamber high up in the center. The odd addition of the so called Air Shafts with small "Alice in Wonderland" doors deep inside and also the purposeful hiding of the lower Shafts by placing building blocks over the outlets and polished granite over the inlets. The centering of the Shafts rather than centering the Doorway and grand Gallery. The concealment of the curious Relieving Chamber rather than including it into the grand design of the Gallery. These are all glaringly complex rather than simple, a plan inside a plan. They do not represent a single purpose of Tomb or Monument. Rather a confusion of intentions or two separate intentions.

The Great Pyramid is a giant leap forward from the normal progression seen in the previous pyramids, nor fully repeated in any later pyramids. But if we remove the 'obvious differences' then it fits nicely into the normal progression of pyramid buildings. The 'obvious differences' were incorporated for a reason other than the usual. Everything I have just mentioned are facts which are not disputed. In my opinion, the conclusion of a Dual Use Theory is the only reasonable conclusion left in the KISS Theorem.

Second Proposal, The Silo and Tomb Design is purely speculation at this time until further discoveries are revealed, but it is a reasonable hypothesis based on both physical evidence and historical text.

A) The Shafts appear to have had a practical purpose rather than religious. If the Shafts served a religious purpose, then only this Pharaoh practiced it for Shafts do not appear in any other pyramid nor is there historical record or rumor of the same. And this one mammoth departure from religious orthodoxy is not accompanied by any others in the same pyramid. The idea that the Shafts were experimental as Air Shafts or Telescope Shafts has a lot more problems than the simpler idea of them being Load Shafts; besides the angle of construction, the manner of construction and the positioning all favor material loading such as cornels. Their approximant 40 degree angle of shaft prefabrication entering the chambers near the floor level with center preference; and do not forget that all the Shaft alterations were left favoring a downward flowing product and of course the small removable door plugs. If we make practicality a requirement for discovering the purpose of the Shafts, considering the huge engineering feat, the labor intensiveness, the originality and the fact they were never improved upon in another pyramid nor evolved from a lesser version in any previous building; then we have to concede they may have been Load Shafts. (Ch.1 section G & H)

B) What else could The Great Pyramid be? The construction is too perfect for a new experiment without specific purpose! The size is to labor intensive for a new experiment without a serious need! The fact that it was built in about 14 years rather than 34 years, that no public buildings were then built to the same scale and innovation, and that the next pyramid tomb attempted to immolate its great forerunner only in size and not interior, all strongly suggest that Pharaoh Khufu was no mad King Ludwig. The facts as we know them in the context of human nature tells me he had a specific purpose and a serious need. (Ch.1 section C & P)

C) Now if we can agree on the 'possibility' of Load Shafts rather than some type of Air Shafts for a Prayer Tower or Soul Escape or Smoke Stack or primitive experiment, then we can also agree on the necessity of more storage space for whatever was being loaded. The Silo design screams out to us. The Middle and Upper Chambers are centered and off-set so that if both chambers extended downward they would be attached front to rear, essentially the same Silo structure. Also the substance coming down the Shafts could be sifted in the ancient manner and simply continue downward for storage. Ancient grain storage in Egypt was essentially a large jar shape space dug underground with a workroom built over top. In The Great Pyramid we are seeing that same design replicated and supersized above ground.

D) The historical Text of Egypt's great famine story makes this Silo idea more than clever imagination! It provides legitimacy to the consideration of a single, well placed, easily managed, Silo structure in Lower Egypt. If that structure took the outward shape of a pyramid, then we could expect it may have been intended to serve as a Pharaoh's Tomb after the long famine was finally over, after the Shafts and Silos had served their purpose. We could expect it because all the pyramids of ancient Egypt were ether used as Tombs or clearly intended as Tombs. And so The Great Pyramid was likely used as a Tomb also. Why else seal and hide the Ascending Corridor, the Upper Burial Chamber before sealing the outside Doorway and hiding its location. My opinion is the Silo and Tomb Design is a reasonable application of the Dual Use Theory.

Third, direct connection between The Great Pyramid and Great Famine must be seriously considered. The great famine story is not owned and copyrighted by religion in the same way the Law of Gravity is not owned by Isaac Newton. The essence of the story is historical from multiple sources, references discovered in Egypt such as on Djoser's Tomb of a seven year famine lend their support that such an event actually happened 4000 years ago even so Djoser seemed to have lived at a different time than Khufu. Howbeit the most detailed and compelling description is from the book of Genesis. Some scoff at anything Biblical, I do not. Remember the author was born and raised in Egypt and he was educated in the royal court of Egypt with access to the famed libraries. Remember also he claims the event took place less than 450 years before he recorded it and his references to all things Egyptian are correct.

The Ancient Text reads; *"Let Pharaoh do this, and let him appoint officers over the land, and take up the fifth part of the land of Egypt in the seven plenteous years. And let them gather all the food of those good years that come, and **lay up corn under the hand of Pharaoh**, and let them keep food in the cities. And that food shall be for store to the land against the seven years of famine, which shall be in the land of Egypt; that the land perish not through the famine. And the thing was good in the eyes of Pharaoh, and in the eyes of all his servants."* Notice this, *"lay up corn under the hand of Pharaoh,"* *"and"* *"let them keep food in the cities."* Clearly there were two plans for storage, under the hand of Pharaoh in one place and in each of the cities. Later in the same text, *"And he gathered up all the food of the seven years, which were in the land of Egypt, and laid up the food in the cities: the food of the field, which was round about every city, laid he up in the same. And Joseph gathered **corn as the sand of the sea, very much**, until he left numbering; for it was without number."* Again we see the purposeful separation, two plans for storage, *"food in the cities,"* *"and"* *"corn as the sand of the sea, very much."*

The story does not mention the Giza Plateau or a Pyramid, but considering so much corn storage in one location with the unusual interior, locale and approximate date of The Great Pyramid, it becomes a serious possibility. The story strongly insinuates the portion of corn collected by Pharaoh was stored in a single place, either a single unit or multiple units in close proximity so that one man could personally supervise its distribution and security, directed by Pharaoh himself. The city of On is mentioned as a side note to the story. The story also insinuates the location to be in a place where foreigners from Canaan could easily approach as they traveled south into Egypt on one of the two major trade routes, both of which met near Giza and the Nile River before it begins to fork apart. These hints could suggest a half dozen places but one of those places would defiantly be Giza-Cairo which is only a few miles from On and located due north of Egypt's Capitol City of Memphis. Don't forget the strange likenesses between Djedef're and Joseph'ra. What do you think, could The Great Pyramid and the Great Famine be connected? (Ch.1 section A)

 Forth, The Escape Tunnel was dugout between 825 and 1650 AD. (Ch.1 section O) **A)** The Tunnel does not reflect the planned uniformity that is plainly seen in the rest of The Great Pyramid. The Descending Passageway and the Ascending Corridor are both set at 26 degree slopes with level hallways into each chamber. The Tunnel is more like a well shaft seen in some underground tombs, but has less of a directional pattern. Its lack of Precise direction is more indicative of an explorer or treasure hunter.

B) The Tunnel is extremely rough and dangerous. One small, skinny person could barely squeeze through it. The Tunnel was cut through the solid rocks of the pyramid, if it were done by the original builders then it was clearly an afterthought that cost a lot of time and served no discernible purpose. Nor does the Tunnel lead to the outside for a complete escape or into the secured Upper Chamber.

C) Its location is also more indicative of an explorer searching a logical hunch. It appears to have been dug down ward from the Middle Chamber hallway through the pyramid structure and all the way to the ground level, then from there in an unsure pattern to exit out the Descending Passageway ceiling. This would be about the same location any person would dig that was searching for a hidden passageway into a secret chamber somewhere between the Middle Chamber and the Basement Chamber, where most pyramid Burial Chambers are found.

D) The Tunnel does reflect the break-in tunnel hammered out by the men of Caliph Mamoun and the short tunnel they hammered around the three granite blocks that secured the Ascending Corridor. We know The Great Pyramid was first broken into by Caliph Abdullah Mamoun about 825 AD and no one reported this escape Tunnel till Professor John Greaves in 1637 AD. Seems perfectly reasonable to suggest someone between Caliph Mamoun and Professor Greaves added this Tunnel to The Great Pyramid.

Fifth, The Relieving Chamber and Gallery was the topside of the first Tower-Crane & Ramp used to raise up the heavy stones seen within the chambers. This is really a natural extension of the Silo theory. It is impossible to determine the degree in which the tallest silo would have been incorporated in raising heavy stones (Ch.1 section M & N). There are a few reasons for proposing it.

A) Because it was available to them. In all their pyramids the basic interior structure was built first. In this case the interior structure was far taller than anything previously constructed. The tower was about 5 to 6 feet thick around each side, because all the Shafts proceed from their inlets horizontally about 6 feet before their intended angle begins. The shorter tower attached to the north side of the taller. The top of the taller was now available to the builders for securing ropes around as a solid pulley.

B) Because they installed the extremely heavy granite wedges at the top. These so called 'false ceilings' or 'relieving beams' are mysteriously notched on the ends and may have been used for long ropes to rap around to a yoke of oxen pulling away while a heavy block moved up the ramp or even up the towers center. Keeping in mind the heaviest blocks in the pyramid are near the ground or near the center tower and all the blocks get much smaller above the tower level.

C) Because the Ascending Corridor and Gallery have a granite floor instead of limestone, the Corridor even has a granite slab ceiling supported by Girdle stones. The granite slabs would be needed for a ramp for dragging up other stone blocks and the 7 unique Girdle stones would serve no unique purpose unless the corridor was originally free standing like a bridge from the ground to the towers top. A picture of the known interior granite tells the story by itself!

D) Finally because the Gallery floor appears to have been built along with the silo tower structure before the pyramid. We can see the Gallery could have proceeded farther up into the Upper & Relieving Chamber. We also see the northern Shafts were bent around the Gallery even so the Shafts are coming from a lower position and are given the primary position in the design and construction. The conflict could have been easily corrected in favor of the Shafts, unless the Gallery-Ramp was already fully constructed beforehand. Experts more experienced then I will determine if this proposal is worthy and make a better argument one way or other.

   Sixth, King and Queen Chambers extend downward beneath the current floor levels into a yet hidden space, just as the Relieving Chamber does. That the hidden Middle-Silo space maybe filled with sand, gravel and old discarded work tools and the hidden Upper-Silo space maybe sectioned into levels with one being the real Burial Chamber.

1) Remember the Relieving Chamber might be called the Revealing Chamber because it reveals the construction design behind the granite coverings of the Upper and Middle Chambers below. It is a natural extension upward of the Upper Chamber hidden above the false ceiling. The Relieving Chamber is also the primary reason we associate The Great Pyramid with Khufu, the actual Great

Pyramid Pharaoh is not yet an absolute fact. The four false ceilings of heavy granite slabs still remain a mystery, but the idea it provided stability and served as the top side of a tower-crane & ramp has merit. Once a person views the Relieving Chamber and the Upper Chamber as the same structure in relation to the Gallery placement, it becomes obvious this same structure likely extends further downward. *Experts have agreed this Relieving Chamber is designed to support itself apart from the surrounding pyramid and designed to support weight for a much larger space below than is currently revealed. (Ch.1 section M)

2) The Upper Chamber is the most stunning, completely finished in tight fitting rose-granite with open Shaft inlets and a Royal Sarcophagus left unsealed and empty. We know the one-piece rose-granite sarcophagus was placed in the chamber during construction because it will not fit threw the chambers only entranceway. So it is equally logical that the chamber walls were covered in the matching rose-granite at the same time, which explains why the Shaft inlets were cut opened threw the rose-granite walls of the Upper Chamber. These Shafts were still being used for corn collection until the last possible harvest before the Great Famine began in earnest. (Ch.1 section L)

3) The smaller Middle Chamber Silo was filled first while the pyramid was being constructed, which explains why these lower Shaft inlets were covered up by the attractive granite slabs of the Middle Chamber walls. The Shaft outlets were also cover by additional layers of stone blocks outside as construction continued past the step pyramid shape. Their little plugs were inserted and the now useless Shafts hidden. Yet the stone floor was left exposed. This would make since if the floor was completed much later after the corn distribution had ended. Also the peeked ceiling and room structure being similar to the Relieving Chamber's peeked ceiling above the Upper Chamber, it is easy to imagine the Middle Chamber could be similarly elongated downward beneath the current floor level as the other was. (Ch.1 section K)

4) The Shafts are extremely fascinating and historically unique. The only practical purpose they could have served is as grainier Load Shafts. Remember the wood pole and bronze rake found inside along with the bronze loop handle on the tiny door plug. The entrances into each of these Chambers is not centered but on one side, nearly along the eastern wall. This purposeful design allowed the Shaft inlets to be centered, both assessable from one side of the floor and creating the possibility for the other side of the floor to be open into a storage area below. (Ch.1 section G & H)

5) Could the center of The Great Pyramid have been hollow below the Load Shaft inlets and current floor levels of the Middle and Upper Chambers, then filled in later with stone slabs, sand gravel, artifacts and even the golden coffin of Pharaoh? The peculiar layout of these Chambers and Shafts inside support the Silo & Tomb Design and become an obvious conclusion once the pyramid's Interior is seen as one-unit minus all the building up around it. Remember, the Exterior was not left unfinished but made beautiful and surrounded by the burial tombs of royal family and friends.

Seventh, Finally this book proposes a Royal Pharaoh is still entombed at the bottom level of the Kings Chamber with his buried treasures; waiting. This is the most risky proposal of the seven, because the others are connected to each other with physical evidence and to start accepting any one of them is to start realizing the others may also be true. But this is separated, because it lacks any written text or physical evidence. But I make the proposal based on four observations.

A) All the other pyramids in Egypt were clearly Tombs or Tomb Markers. The Great Pyramid has differences but not so different to think it was intended to end up as anything but a Tomb. Also it was attached by a path to a Mortuary Temple and surrounded by lesser Tombs.

B) The fact that The Great Pyramid was closed and sealed. It is hard to imagine they would have lowered those three 7 ton granite blocks across the Ascending Corridor to painstakingly seal entry or sealed the Antechamber into the Upper Burial Chamber or laid those beautiful rose-granite floor tiles in the same Burial Chamber before closing up and hiding the Doorway from the outside if no one had been entombed inside.

C) In all the other Pyramid Tombs the Pharaoh is buried underneath or slightly above ground level. It would seem unnatural for this Pharaoh to be buried suspended so high above ground. Rather he would be carried up to the Upper Kings Chamber then lowered down the Silo tower to the bottom along with his personal treasures. Likely this bottom chamber would have been sealed about in heavy granite. *He was laid to rest at the same relative locale as all the other burial chambers of his Dynasty, only his was accessed from the above rather than below!

D) Maybe the Caliph did find the Pharaoh and his stuff inside the Kings Chamber, but chose to hide his discovery. Maybe Pharaoh decided at the last minute to be buried in a separate secreted chamber or he was so hated that priest dumped his body down a hole and sealed the pyramid as if he was inside. But if the floors are false and both Chambers really extend downward, then who can tell what artifacts have been sitting in them for all this time. Who can say if Lord Pharaoh, maybe Khufu/Cheops himself is comfortable resting in an open space beneath the floor of the Upper Chamber, smiling at the thousands of people for thousands of years walking over his Tomb. Who can say if the *long rumored Library of the world's most ancient books being hidden nearby may be true, hidden in one of these silo spaces and preserved as well as the solar ships discovered below. I suspect and hope he will be discovered far below the extended Kings Chamber in his gold coffin surrounded by his personal treasures, text and one other item, which I do not mentioned anywhere in this book.

The Great Pyramid Mystery. <u>But this mystery could be solved one day soon</u>. Archaeologists, Historians and Egyptologist have been getting closer and closer each year. The ideas put forth here will help and the Experiment will prove which direction to move forward. Whatever truth may be discovered, The Great Pyramid of Giza Egypt is an Honorable Accomplishment and memorial to a great Royal Family of the past and to a great and ancient Nation of the present.

Part Two = THE EXPERIMENT: Proven by scientific method?

Egyptian relief showing hungry nomads begging bread

To prove the Dual Use Theory and the Silo & Tomb Intent of The Great Pyramid which could explain all the mysteries associated with The Great Pyramid, we would need to perform a quick, non intrusive test. A Simple Drill Test. Take a 1" x 10' drill bit, nearly 1 inch diameter Carbide Tipped Bit with a Hammer Drill made for drilling holes in stone, that is sectioned to about 10 foot in length attached to a portable stabilizing frame to guide the dill straight and steady. With permission and direction from the Egyptian Ministry of Antiquities, drill a single small hole down into the floor of the Middle Chamber and another into the floor of the Upper Chamber. This small drilled hole would preserve the ancient structure from unwanted damage while allowing researchers to determine if there was empty space under these floors. Also the hole could be simply filled in with plaster making the small spot on the floor unnoticed to all visitors.

A) Drill one 1 inch hole 10 foot down into the floor of the Upper Chamber. Choose a spot two paces West of center from the Shaft inlets and the room's center. Again this side should have been opened into the continuing space below with the remainder of the stone floor added later.

The drill bit will need to neatly penetrate the beautiful rose-granite floor covering and possibly two solid stone blocks beneath. The drill bit should enter a space hidden below a false floor. I expect the drill bit will enter a chamber continuation with nearly equal diminutions as the Upper Chamber and the Relieving Chamber because it will just be an extension downward of the same. The first section of space could be filled with sand gravel and the Silo will likely be divided into granite sections similar to those of the Relieving Chamber above. But it would still prove the chambers Sneferu-Pattern, with both the design and intent for The Great Pyramid. Of course if the evidence connection presented here is wrong such as forcing a round ball into an oval hole, then the drill bit should meet solid stone all ten feet.

B) Drill one 1 inch hole 10 foot down into the floor of the <u>Middle Chamber</u>. Choose a spot two paces West of center from the Shaft Inlets and the room's center, other side from entrance. This side of the floor should have been opened into the continuing space below with the remainder of the stone floor added later. The drill will need to neatly penetrate the stone floor and possibly two stone blocks beneath. The drill bit should enter sand and gravel used to fill the Silo space along with discarded tools and corn baskets, similar to what <u>Colonel Howard Vyse</u> reported hidden below this floor. Also drill a single 1 inch hole into the rear South wall high up near the ceiling base, between the South wall's Shaft inlet and the West wall, to determine if and how far down the Upper Chamber may extend. If for example one may have drained into the other.

C) Other holes could be drilled in the interest of discovery, such as in the <u>Basement Chamber's</u> center ceiling below the tower, or above the curious right side wall, or in the dead end passageway. Another quick, non intrusive test would be to collect <u>dust samples</u> from deep inside the Shafts and have them analyzed for hints of grain.

In the 1800's researchers used big hammers and small sticks of dynamite in and around The Great Pyramid to discover hidden tunnels. This is how the false ceiling of the Upper Chamber was discovered, exposing the secret Relieving Chamber and the word "Khufu". This is how the Shafts in the Middle Chamber were first discovered behind the granite coverings. They also blasted sideways into some of the Shafts thinking they might connect to other rooms. And even a small tunnel down through the foundation. If they would have realized the layout we know today with the Middle and Upper Chambers offset above and below, with the precise angles of the uniformed Shafts, and with the Relieving Chamber's structural design extending the Upper Chamber's natural height, they would have likely realized enough to also blast part of the floor beneath the Chambers.

Today no one wants to cause anymore damage to The Great Pyramid, first of the Seven Wonders of the World. That is why a long, thin drill hole is a good idea, it should cause no damage to the pyramid's structural stability, to the preservation of its antiquity, nor to its tourism value. The Drill Test would be a sensible approach to solving many questions related to The Great Pyramid. After experts have discussed all the evidence in relation to The Dual Use Theory and in context of the Silo & Tomb Design, then maybe Shaft dust samples could be analyzed and a simple Drill Test could be professionally done, both with very great interest. I dearly wish to be present for the Drill Test. It is always a pleasure to see the *wonderful men and women that do the hard work of painstakingly revealing the historical facts one by one over the years till suddenly the truth becomes plain. And sometimes plain truth is surprising.

Part Three = History of Ancient Egypt in Brief Outlines.

An Egyptian Priest named <u>Manetho</u> wrote a <u>History of Egypt</u> in 250 BC which he lists 31 Dynasties from Menes to the conquest of Alexander the Great. Egyptian history has been divided this way ever sense. The seven divisions, dates and notes are the most commonly excepted references. It is possible some of these Dynasties were concurrent with each other rather than consecutive between the Capitols of Memphis, Thebes and Tanis while others controlled all, which would reduce the dates. It is just as possible these Dynasties and dates are essentially correct.

1. First Egyptian Period $1^{st} - 2^{nd}$ Dynasties   3000 – 2700 BC or 2500 – 2300 BC (BCE)

The historical records are rare and vague.   <u>Mysraim</u> is believed by many to be the father of Egypt. He possessed the 'Right of Eldest Son of the Eldest Son' and therefore would have been seen by many as the senior ruler among the whole world of men. According to Moses, Noah's eldest son was Ham and Ham's eldest was Canaan whom received a curse instead elevating Ham's second son, *"And Mysraim begat Ludim, and Anamim, and Lehabim, and Naphtuhim, and Pathrusim, and Casluhim, and Caphtorim."* <u>Menes</u> is considered the first king of Greater Egypt, his tomb was discovered along with others of his family in Abydos which is northeast of Thebes.

2. Old Kingdom Period $3^{rd} - 6^{th}$ Dynasties   2700 – 2200 BC or 2200 – 1900 BC (BCE)

The historical records are vague, most accounts were written much later. Capitol City is in **Memphis**. This is the pyramid era, including <u>The Great Pyramid</u> of Giza. During this time ships were built and sent into the Mediterranean Sea, cities were progressed and huge mortuary temples honored dead Pharaohs. Supposedly OKP began with the 3rd Dynasty Family of <u>Djoser</u> and ended with the 6th Dynasty Family of <u>Pepi</u>. I believe this is when <u>Abraham</u> visited and later <u>Jacob</u> settled in Egypt. A great famine is referenced during this Period by many sources.

3. **First Intermediate Period**   7th – 10th Dynasties   2100 – 2000 BC (BCE)

The historical records are vague. There were hard changes taking place as a glorious Old Kingdom breaks apart and fades away.

4. **Middle Kingdom Period**   11th – 12th Dynasties   1900 – 1700 BC (BCE)

The historical record begins to take on more detailed shape. Capitol City moved primarily to **Thebes**. During this time a canal was built from the Nile River to the Red Sea, they also built up cities and monuments and expanded the Kingdom, partly with slave labor. The 11th Dynasty Family of Amenemhet I (Charlemagne) established a powerful new government and 12th Dynasty Family of Senusert I built the Obelisk of On. MKP could also be called the First Empire Period. I believe this is the time of Hebrew slavery and Moses, others believe this is when Abraham visited. A lot depends on your interpretation of the official 31 Dynasties and which dating process you are persuaded of.

5. **Second Intermediate Period**   13th – 17th Dynasties   1700 – 1600 BC (BCE)

Asiatic Hyksos, Sheppard Kings seized control of half the country during this period. Capitol City moved to **Tanis** in the Delta. They ruled for an hundred years but are considered unpopular. I believe this is the result of the Exodus, others believe this is when Joseph and Jacob settled in Egypt. Constant change and rebellions would have made it a very tough time. A famine is referenced.

6. **New Kingdom Period**   18th – 20th Dynasties   1600 – 1100 BC (BCE)

The historical record becomes more detailed here in Egypt and around the world. Capitol City moved back to **Thebes**. Thotmes, Amenhotep and Ramses Dynasties ruled with power, dominating from Ethiopia to Syria to the Euphrates. They built cities and repaired monument across Egypt, partly with slave labor. NKP could also be called the Second Empire Period; the world's first superpower. I believe this is the time of the Judges and Kings, others believe this is the time of Moses, if so then no Egyptian record of him has yet survived this period.

7. Post Empire Period $21^{st} – 31^{st}$ Dynasties   1000 – 30 BC (BCE)

Egyptian Nationalism; Assyrian then Persian dominance; Greek then Roman dominance; Turkish then Arabic dominance; French then British dominance, and now the Egyptian Republic . . . The Persian Era lasted from 525 to 332 BC. Alexander the Great came in 332 BC and built Alexandria Egypt, the Ptolemaic Era lasted from 304 to 30 BC. Julius Caesar laid siege to Alexandria in 48 BC, and fell in love with Egypt's Cleopatra. Today Egypt is one of the most interesting tourist destinations on earth.

Another Outline of Ancient Egypt may be presented as such:

A] Settlement Period   Extended tribes of Mysraim settle the land along the Nile River by Chieftains. The land greener than today, connecting two land masses and two seas makes a perfect location for hunting, gathering, farming and trade.

B] Original Kingdom Period   Civilization, social law and justice, wealth and security all increase with the rise of the Original Kingdom. Rising of **Memphis** as the Capitol City. Establishing of dynastic royalty, cast systems and orthodox religion. Forging the first Nation as strong city-states are emerging in Nubia, Canaan and Babylon.   Ruling classes are generally Hamitic as social evolution leaps forward then stops. Includes the pyramid era.

C] National Kingdom Period   Overthrow of the original dynastic royalty and establishment of another causing changes in the cast system and orthodox religion. Rise of **Thebes** as a Capitol City. Ruling classes are racially diversified. Nation building and Civilization in Egypt leaps forward again then stops again. First Empire Period.

D] Divided Kingdom Period   Lower Egypt conquered by invaders. Rise of **Tanis** as a Capital City. Also the Divided Kingdom Period occasionally applies during the Original Kingdom and Nation Kingdom as Lower and Upper Egypt seem to have occasionally tested each other's resolve.

E] United Kingdom Period Egypt is permanently reunited. Its National Kingdom reestablished from **Thebes**. Its former wealth, power and civilization fully recovered. Second Empire Period.

F] Proxy Kingdom Period A series of invasions by a series of foreign Empires finally leaves a weakened Egypt governed by the Ptolemaic Pharaohs and Proxy Governors. The end of the Pharaohs and the old religions fade away during this period.

G] New Republic Period The modern emergence of Egyptian Army and Civilian Representative government. Regional stability and leadership.

The current religion is primarily Muslim Islamic and then Coptic Christianity by influence; with the common variety of personal religious beliefs and sects.

Biblical Chronology and The Great Pyramid is an interesting subject of its own. This connection of the Bible's Great Famine and Egypt's Great Pyramid will fit neatly into Biblical Chronology and Egyptian History with minor Time Line adjustments. The Bible states 430 years (Exodus 12:40) from entering Egypt during the second year of famine to exiting Egypt; and 480 years (Kings 6:1) from exiting Egypt to starting construction on Solomon's Temple. *That is 910 years from Joseph's Famine to Solomon's Temple. The key to fixing the Time Line could be as simple as proving the likely connection between the Great Famine and The Great Pyramid of Giza.

The First Question, is there historical events also documented in the Biblical text which happened in both Egypt and Israel to establish a reliable time line. Nebuchadnezzar lead an army out of Babylon, about 600's BC, he destroyed Jerusalem and conquered Israel during the time of 'Jeremiah' and 'Daniel'. The same army also conquered Egypt after the New Kingdom Period (United Kingdom Period). If correct, would place King Solomon and his Temple of 'I Kings' about the early New Kingdom Period and Joseph and his Famine late Old Kingdom.

The Second Question a person must answer for themselves is whether The Great Pyramid was built before or after the great deluge. Currently some Scholars believe The Great Pyramid and its neighbor Kafre's pyramid were built before, in spite the lack of real evidence. But I would suggest the argument has been made here in Chapter One and numerous other books that it was built after the flood. *Even Egyptian tradition states a great flood had destroyed the world before the 1st Dynasty. Also the Biblical account of the flood plainly states not only rain fell but the deep was broken up. Likely no buildings from the previous age survived into ours unless they were broken into pieces and buried in soot. Despite rumors, The Great Pyramid would not have been water tight submerged under water, because of the upper Shaft outlets. Some other scholars suggest the Hebrew slaves built it, but the Bible plainly says they built cities with mud bricks and mortar, of which The Great Pyramid has none.

The Third Question, is when did the great deluge (Flood) happen. According to Halley's Bible Handbook, the historic beginning of the two oldest civilizations, Babylonia and Egypt is variously placed between 5000 BC and 2300 BC. This is an averaging of leading Historians. The current historic opinion is about 3100 BC for both. The Biblical flood date according to the English about 2500-2300 BC, according to the Septuagint about 3300 BC, and according to the Samaritan Pentateuch about 3000 BC. The difference in time is minor considering the more amazing fact that the flood dates are so similar to the current historic date for the two oldest civilized City-States. And both these Cities-States claimed to have emerged after such a flood. Civilized Egypt would have begun about 100 years after this flood/late ice age, as tribes and clans established social trade cities.

The Forth Question is which Pharaohs challenged Moses. A Pharaoh of Egypt turned against the Hebrew tribes, making them a slave class and attempted to slay all male new born children. Another Pharaoh challenged Moses leadership and endured ten plagues. Many believe Thotmes III and Amenhotep II of the New Kingdom Period may have been the Pharaohs of the Exodus. Many others believe Rameses II and Merneptah also of the New Kingdom Period may have been the Pharaohs of the Exodus. Both sets have one or two interesting discoveries that suggest their connection, but all four mummies have been found and are on display in Museum. *Exodus 15 suggest that Pharaoh himself drown in the Red Sea, *"For the horse of Pharaoh went in with his chariots and with his horsemen into the sea, and the Lord brought again the waters of the sea upon them;"* The historical record during Egypt's NKP does not even hint of this event or the ten plagues. The historical record is fairly good. The occasional Pharaoh was so despised that his or her name was scratched off official records and monument yet Egyptologist still know a fair amount about them, but nothing about Joseph or Moses survives in this period. Likely these men lived long before the NKP in a different part of the country and their events had already entered into mythology. In fact the first king of the New Kingdom Period may be named after Moses, Pharaoh Ahmosis.

*I grew up in the United States only two hundred years after the Revolutionary War but the world is a different place and I would not have any clue it ever happened accept for some history books, a few scatted monuments and all the people named Washington, Adams, Franklin, Hamilton, Jefferson and so on. The same is true for people thousands of years ago about events only two hundred years previous, and most of them lacked access to books.

*The uncovered NKP letters from Canaan asking for help, "or the whole land will be lost to Pharaoh" may not be referring to Joshua's Invasion of Canaan but rather King David's Conquest. Pharaoh does not send help and later his daughter marries David's son, King Solomon. *And the boast of Rameses, "Israel is no more" may simply be Pharaoh's famous victory over Jerusalem and pillage of the Temple in II Kings. These obscure NKP references applied correctly would push the time of Joseph back to the OKP and the time of Moses back to the MKP.

If The Great Pyramid was also a giant corn silo built for the seven year famine, then Joseph served the Old Kingdom in Memphis. But Moses served the Middle Kingdom Empire, which knew not Joseph, in Thebes. Here slave labor replaced some of the peasant class laborers and Pharaohs switched from building pyramids to great public works. When Pharaoh and all his captains unexpectedly drowned in the Red Sea, Egypt was suddenly vulnerable and the government overthrown. Soon ravaged by civil war and invasion of the Second Intermediate

Period (Divided Kingdom Period), a new dynasty rises to power in Thebes. The new Israel settled into Canaan without interference from Egypt.   Remember Josephus the Jewish Historian that lived during the time of Jesus Christ, he suggested the Seven Year Famine may have happened during the early MKP, but not the NKP, for a reference he had found referring to seven empty years but he was not sure.   But the discovery of the Famine Stela mentioned in Chapter One, referred to the Seven Year Famine during the OKP, the pyramid age.

[The new NKP dynasty attached the "mosis" to their name.   Interesting consideration: was the new Dynasty able to rise because the power of their former political/family rival was broken by Moses?   Or could it be possible the young man Moses bare royal children in Egypt before fleeing his angry Pharaoh Step-father?   Finally, could the historical Djedef're be our Joseph?]   Hmmm

The Eye of Ra and The Great Pyramid are stamped on the back of the USA one dollar bill. We know it is The Great Pyramid because of its perfect summitry and because it does not have a cap stone, rather an all seeing eye. Symbols of the Masons and a host of secretive societies throughout history. Symbolizing the relationship between the earth below, God above and mankind focused upwards. *Likely the pyramid symbolized the Hope and Religion of the Early Egyptians of Antiquity. Later evolving into the cult of Re.

A) Consider the name Israel is one of the many names of God which he gave to Jacob during Egypt's Pyramid Age. Interestingly the one name consist of three root words, IS-RA-EL.   IS = God, The Eternal, The Spirit; Apis, Horus, Osiris, Isis, Permethis, Isabel, Ishmael, Islam to name a few are derivatives of the primitive root word.   RA (sometimes Re or Ru) = God, The All Seeing, All Knowing; MysRa, Ra'amah, Rameses, AbRam, Ramadan, 'Eye of Ra' was likely a reference to the sun as the light from God's Eye always watching; the supreme God having no form.   EL = God, The Creator, Holy One; Elohim, Elam, El'Bethel, El'Kab, Bael, and so on of the primitive root word. Three are One.

B) Consider that raw historical facts (minus the commentaries) from around the world can support the idea that ancient men and women of antiquity, more than four thousand years ago may have generally viewed God in the singular as "all seeing", "judging mortal deeds" and were not so much image worshippers or detailed polytheist. Sure Osiris and Horus are referenced on Old Kingdom pyramid text, but few if any idols or alters appear suggesting they were then lesser of RA, archangel demigod types. *Sir Flinders Petrie of the British Museum also agreed that monotheism (One God with lesser angelic-types) was clearly the religion of primitive mankind from Babylon to Egypt.

C) Also consider that Ishmael's mother was Egyptian chosen by Abraham and Sara, Abraham being a prophet. That an Old Kingdom Pharaoh feared committing adultery. And that God warned another Old Kingdom Pharaoh of the Great Famine. That two tribes of Israel descend from the Egyptian wife of Joseph. That Pharaoh would accept blessing from the old prophet Jacob. That Moses was restoring the "old religion" of Jacob and rejected the images and polytheism that had since evolved in Egypt. And that the prophets Isaiah and Zechariah predicted a future age when Egypt and Israel will have a strong alliance and become the world's foremost nations, and said *"Egypt my people and Israel my chosen"*. That the child Jesus Christ the Lord lived in Egypt for a time and confirmed those prophets. And even the prophet Muhammad said he was restoring the "old religion" of Ishmael and rejected the images and polytheism that had since evolved in Arabia. Suggesting Image worship and polytheism evolved from basic monotheism, not vise versa.

D) Conclusion, all these points suggest that many ancient people believed Egypt's Old Kingdom Religion early on may have had a similar monotheistic view of God as ours. For us this means an Old Kingdom Pharaoh could have been motivated to do the impossible and the improbable by dreams and visions, even to build a stone Ark against a flood of Famine. Same God yesterday, today and forever.

Remember the Dual Use Theory and the Silo & Tomb Design are reasonable concepts based on both physical evidences and historical texts.   ONE, visualizing the center chambers as an independent structure with the corridor as an attached support ramp. Agreeing the whole chamber structure was built first will create the space needed inside for the amount of corn required and the independent levels for sealing that corn. More than 146,200 cubic feet. Remember the other pyramid chambers were built first. The peaked roof over each chamber with a false ceiling vertically extending one chamber and the 6 foot walls which barely off-set the two chambers and allow them to stand as an independent structure.

TWO, accepting the Shafts had a practical use, this must eventually lead to the Load Shaft conclusion for a small solid substance. They were used during and not after the final pyramid construction. Remember the inlets are nearly floor level, centered, with the lower Shafts covered and ending about 25 foot short for a step pyramid phase while the upper Shafts uncovered and exiting. The 38 to 40 degree downward angle with removable door-plugs. The shaft tools and internal scratches across the joints.

THREE and finally, considering the Ancient Text suggestion that corn was gathered from across the nation into one place under the Hand of Pharaoh. Remember the location is appropriate in every way and the sudden increase in wealth and power is notable. Pretend for a moment that it might be true and see all the mysterious discoveries related to The Great Pyramid fit neatly into place.

Proof positive is only a Drill Test away. Will the drill bit reach through the thick chamber floors and find open silo space continuing downward with sand gravel, ancient tools, artifacts and treasures. Or will it only meet solid stone after solid stone. The circumstantial evidence is compelling in our favor of the chamber-tower. The proper Drill and bit is such a nonintrusive method to explore and discover secretive chambers in buildings like The Great Pyramid of Giza. Once a working theory has been discussed for probable credibility and measures procured to seal the holes after a small camera has been inserted and results documented; then exploration and preservation both move forward together. In this case proof positive is only a Drill Test away! Historical records at this time period are scarce. Clearly records were not preserved if they mentioned specific monuments and famous deeds of this Royal Fourth Dynasty because the powerful new Pharaohs that eventually replaced them had different dreams for the future of Egypt. The Old Kingdom past away. Today, truth is stranger than fiction, but even when it is not, it is still preferable.

The Great Pyramid Mystery is already Egypt's most popular attraction. Discovering the silo spaces hidden inside will be a big story. But if ancient artifacts, old books or even the Great Pharaoh himself is found inside then it will be one of the biggest human interest events in modern history. Every teacher and student, tourist and vacationer will have to return to Cairo! Jewish tourist will want to touch the spot where their twelve forefathers stood together for the first time. Christian tourist will walk about in groups to see an event straight out of the Bible. Muslim tourist will marvel at what their ancestors did wholly surrendered to the Will of God. And every Scientist of antiquity will have to examine the man-made wonders of The Great Pyramid again. Everything Egyptian will be back in vogue!

But more importantly, a primary turning point in our human social evolution will be exposed. The Egyptian people stood up together, moved mountains and saved themselves. Mankind had been sufficiently motivated by God to create something brand new. Inspiration spread around the world from seeing the wonder of The Great Pyramid and the human consciousness expanded. People began to dream of new construct possibilities.

Egypt

- International boundary
- ★ National capital
- Railroad
- Road

0 50 100 150 Kilometers
0 50 100 150 Miles

Crete (GR.)

Mediterranean Sea

CYPRUS ★ Nicosia
Limassol
Tartūs
Ḥimṣ
Tripoli
LEBANON
Beirut ★
SYRIA
★ Damascus
UNDOF Zone
GOLAN HEIGHTS*
Haifa
ISRAEL
Irbid
Tel Aviv-Yafo
WEST BANK*
Jerusalem
Amman
1967 Cease-Fire Line
GAZA STRIP*
Beersheba
Al 'Arīsh
1949 Armistice Line
JORDAN
Ma'ān

Bardīyah
As Sallūm
Marsá Maţrūḥ
Damietta
Port Said
Alexandria
Kafr ash Shaykh
Damanhūr
Ţanţā
Al Manşūrah
Az Zaqāzīq
Banhā
Shibīn al Kawm
Ismailia
Suez Canal
LIBYA
Al Jaghbūb
Al Jīzah ★ Cairo
Suez
Ḥulwān
Sinai
Siwah
Al Fayyūm
Bani Suwayf
Al Bawīţī
Al Minyā
Ra's Ghārib
Al Ţūr
Eilat
Al 'Aqabah
Ḥaql
Tabūk
SAUDI ARABIA
Asyūţ
Sharm ash Shaykh
Al Ghurdaqah
Sūhāj
Bûr Safājah
Qinā
Al Quşayr
Al Wajh
Mūţ
Luxor
Al Khārijah
Red Sea
Bārīs
Aswān High Dam
Aswān
Mīnā' Barānīs
Lake Nasser
Administrative Boundary
Halā'ib
Wādī Ḥalfā'
Dungunāb

*The Golan Heights is Israeli-occupied Syria, the West Bank and Gaza Strip are Israeli occupied with status to be determined. Boundary representation

SUDAN

CHAPTER THREE   KHUFU'S GOLD:

"The Power of a Great Idea in the hands of Determined Men" SSD

1} ADVENTURE BEGINS & THE GIZA MEETING   2} REBELS IN THE CAMP &
THE KING IS DEAD-LONG LIVE THE KING   3} BITTER-SWEET & KHUFU'S GOLD

Part One = ADVENTURE BEGINS

[One month into the Giza Project]   Pharaoh awoke suddenly; sweat was pouring from his forehead; where was that cup of water that was always to be next to his bed. Darkness was still pouring in the small window flap of his tent but the light breeze had obviously stopped sometime while he was sleeping. He felt around the floor next to his royal bed mat; Ah, there it was, and he drank fully.

Pharaoh, king of Egypt, rich, famous, powerful and descendant of the blood royal, sat up in the warm darkness and drank the cool water. Ah, it was good. He was reviewing in his mind the two dreamy visions that had suddenly changed all his future plans. Odd dreams, more like a visitation. Now he knew there would be no invasions east or west. His army had been summoned here, to the Giza Plateau. He, Pharaoh, had seen into the future and he planned to be ready for it

Pharaoh was what men called the top side of middle-aged, and he was starting to feel it. He was regular height and build with the dark skin and black frizzled hair and the strong features of his noble race. His constitution had always been healthy and strong but lately he had started to feel it, whatever it was, who knew. Hopefully just hard work and age finally catching up together. He had ruled Egypt like his father, with a strong and steady hand. He had personally led his army to secure rebellious provinces, expanded trade and crafts, expanded schools of learning. This early morning Pharaoh set down the cup next to his gold dagger and lay back, head slightly tilted up by a duck feathered pillow sowed into rabbit furs. Ten years ago I would have brought one of my younger wives on a trip like this just to cuddle up, he thought with a barely perceptible smirk, but now I prefer the solitude. Funny how we change over time; I wonder do we actually get smarter with time or are we just as smart as ever and become a different person with time. Ah, I will ask the Court Magicians that tomorrow, it will keep them busy for awhile deciding which answer would please me more, "AH, HA HA;" a little chuckle actually vocalized itself aloud at that thought.

The tent was large of badger skin and heavy with thick hand woven rugs carpeted across the floor. Six side by side elephant hides were stretched underneath the luxurious rugs for matting against the hard rock of the great plateau outside, a place called Giza. Waves of soft wool curtains decorated the interior tent walls embroider with the resting lion with head erect and alert, on backgrounds of differing shades of green and yellow edged with fine wires of real gold. Each curtain gracefully draped down then waved up to overlap the next, the greens and yellows creating an oasis atmosphere. Pharaoh was King of Egypt as his fathers before him, and his family had ruled parts of Upper and Lower Egypt from Memphis for many years. He was determined to finally surmount the political and ethnic difficulties to mold the whole 'Two Lands' into one people, one enduring Nation. He bemused, surely no man in all the world ruled such a vast territory of citizens with so many cities and towns since the time of Noe. Of course those Merchants of rare goods from the Far East reported news of a similar thing there, but no matter, his was first, his was greatest, his was Egypt. RA had declared long ago that Egypt was his people and so surely it was so.

The cedar wood poles set around not only supported the weight of the tent but also hooked long boards from one pole to the other for added support and beauty with ornate hieroglyphs and depictions of his family exploits. Also from them hung various clothes of State and leisure, weapons and domestic tools. His short curved sword with silver handle topped with the blood red ruby, his mother had given it to him years ago when he had gone to fight in his first battle. His set of three matching water jugs of rarest quality that Mother asked him to keep in her memory. She was a strong hard woman in her time, but Ah, how he missed her. Hanging in the corner was his leather war armor with squares of greenish bronze sown into the fabric. Next to that his collection of short spears, each perfectly balanced for long flight and quick death. His pouches of coin. His writing inks and feathers; it was these he reached for after raising to light two great candle bowls on the cedar wood table located to the tent's front and center.

"IS ALL WELL, MY PHARAOH?" Came the voice of Tiche No, Captain of the Royal Guard from outside the tent. "All is well." Pharaoh replied as he spread out the survey sheets of the Giza Plateau and examined them yet again. His plans for the plateau were bold, so bold he had not missed in his peripheral vision the skeptical looks from his royal engineer. But the Chief Engineer had over stepped when he dared to explain to his Pharaoh the impossibility of such an enterprise; fool, nothing is impossible only impractical. Let him reflect on that from the prison cell till I decide whether he should be reinstated or beheaded.

Of course ether decision would be acceptable, Pharaoh knew. His Chief Butler is twice as good as before and his new Chief Baker is a notable improvement from the former. A few years back the Chief Butler and the Chief Baker had both offended him and were cast into prison. The Baker's head was removed and set out for the birds to dine on, and the Butler was reinstated to his duties. That was on my birthday celebrations, Pharaoh remembered. I had always liked that Butler, my sister's relation; both good decisions. The great Pharaoh scratched his head then massaged his temples, I'll wait and see how creative my Engineering Staff are and their so called 'Mathematics' and my Magicians and Mystics and their so called 'Sciences' and oh, my Philosophers, Astrologers, Inventors, Poets and Seers, all of whom lead about students and eat my bread for the privilege to provide good Counsel to the Royal Family. Hmm how big should the corn silos be? How many will we need? How do we protect them? And what about style, cost? It must have style. Pharaoh moved his finger across the survey lines. His Great Sphinx was nearly completed, facing north toward Canaan's land, toward the sea and the trade routes, toward Egypt's future and IT HAD STYLE. I have built a wonder here on the high plateau and I shall build more wonders here, he mused. All who see know they have entered into a great county among a great people, from barbarism into civilization. Pharaoh smiled to himself, the Sphinx Lion body was huge and forbidding. The head erect and alert was his own, the likeness not displeasing.

The location here was perfect, it came to him during the first planning meetings less than a month ago. Discussions with his Senior Lords of the Empire on how to proceed with the Divine Revelation, seven years of plenty followed by seven years of severe famine and time was already counting down. Here on the northern plateau along the Nile River and Trade Routes, he could build a fortress or maybe a new distribution center where more Egyptian Tradesmen could buy in bulk and more tariff taxes could be collected and more Egyptian workers moving goods throughout the country, reducing again the number of large foreign caravans still wondering about. Pharaoh felt a new sense of purpose, he was tasked direct from Ra to save Egypt and the more he worked the task the more he realized the huge potential.

He had been focused on securing the differing political factions of Upper and Lower Egypt to Memphis control and assessing the treasury to finance his east and westward expansions while maintaining a peace with the Nubian kingdoms southward. But suddenly, by divine intervention, he was tasked with a holy duty, a test. Only now was Pharaoh beginning to understand that Ra had provided the solution to all his problems with a single stroke of nature. His enemies, domestic and foreign did not know what he knew! The two dreamy visions were clear, seven years of plenty would be followed by seven years of extreme famine. AH, he would be prepared and they would not. He would have food and they would not. Pharaoh smiled again to himself. The candle bowls burned. He knew an opportunity when he saw it.

The morning sun peeked bright across the desert sand, the sandstone plateau and shimmering a golden fog about the Nile River as it's rays passed west against the distant hills. Father and Son, a Pharaoh and a Prince finished the last bits of their breakfast together. This morning was scrambled eggs mingled with strips of toasted bread and thin crunchy bits of seasoned alligator meat, tiny pinches of greens topped with small chunks of fruit jam. Prince Khufu picked up his plate to lick the remaining smudges when his mascara eyes drifted up over the plate's edge to see Pharaoh glaring him.   "Sorry my Father," he said, quickly lowering the plate away from his face and setting it back on the table. Pharaoh put a pinch of sugar into his water and stirred it once with his finger before drinking, "My son, remember you are a Prince of Egypt. Here your father again and remember the virtues of maturity from your lessons. Always virtues must subdue desires, even as knowledge subdues innocence."   "Yes my Father."   "Think before you act, my son."   "Yes my Father."   Pharaoh sighed, "Ah, go my son and play with your fellows till the sun reaches the second quarter then return here with a full display of your maturity. Quietly observe the meeting that will be in progress."   "Yes my Father," Khufu said a bit more enthusiastically as he leapt up and darted out the tent flaps.   Pharaoh sighed again shaking his head; then seeing his son was gone, he lifted his own plate and licked off the fruity smudges.

Today he hoped to approve all final plans, and commission the work to begin. Maybe he did want to be entombed here after all. Hmmm, why not next to my beautiful Sphinx. Well it was time to begin a long day, an expansive day and the Eye of Ra was already growing large and unblinking in the morning sky.

THE GIZA MEETING

"WHAT ARE YOU SAYING?! THAT IT CAN NOT BE DONE?! THAT IT IS IMPOSSIBLE?! IS THAT WHAT YOU ARE SAYING TO ME?!" Pharaoh screamed out, slamming his fist into the table.   IutuoHamic suddenly fell to his knees, "No No Lord, not impossible, nothing is impossible, nothing."

Pharaoh glared at him bowed low, "then tell me again what you ARE saying Tutuo." TutuoHamic for his part remained on his knees bowed low judging the Pharaohs mood was still dangerous, "My Pharaoh", Tutuo began, "Seer of Divine visions and most favored son of heaven; so much corn for so many years should not be stored by just enlarging the usual granary design set underground, they would have to be set above the ground, but we astrologers agree with the Magicians whom have also determined that our current granary design would have to be changed if it is to be above ground. The design will have to be changed, that is what we are saying, the design will have to be changed if we set them above ground." Hudene spoke out, " Lord Pharaoh, the traditional granary works and is proven, I still think we should just honeycomb the entire Plateau with a hundred thousand proper grain holes and be done with it."

Pharaoh relaxed his countenance and looked to Hudene. Hudene was the Chief Magician, an independent mind and old fashion in every way, a good balance to Pharaohs many grand ideas, but Pharaoh was also aware Hudene did not much believe in a coming famine and had a 'wait to see attitude'. Tutuo stood up and also looked to Hudene along with the other Counselors. Pharaoh set back into a business mode, "We may not have a choice at the end of the day, but I do not like it. This is a task from the most high God and I want it to be worthy of the task." Pharaoh paused as he looked out the open Tent flaps beyond the guards that stood rigidly alert to the great expanse of the plateau beyond. "It is not grand, I want something grand, something for the whole world to gaze and wonder at the might of Egypt and the glory of Ra." The room inside the Royal tent was silent for a moment. This time Polohamic spoke, he was the Chief Priest, a heavy set man with dropping face and practical about everything, especially meal times, "Have our engineers discovered a way to construct hollow pyramids for the corn?" Pharaoh shrugged, "Zaph'nathpaane'ah and the engineering team have not arrived yet, I sent soldiers out this morning to find them." Zaph known as Joseph, was the mysterious Chief Governor recently appointed by Pharaoh and said to possess the power of divination. "Honored King," TutuoHamic began thoughtfully wanting back in the discussion, "these pyramid silos would have to be quite sizable." "Yes I agree and seven sizable pyramids, one for each year of famine." Polohamic said.   Pharaoh stepped back and gazed into the middle distance attempting to picture seven large pyramids set, how, across the plateau, "Ah" he murmured aloud, "I like that, lay them out with the stars above, maybe the Big Dipper." He said with a smile.

Khufu stepped into the tent opening just then, "MY LORD PHARAOH! Zaph's caravan has arrived with the engineers from Memphis and someone is KILLED!" Everyone just turned and stared at young Khufu for a moment as the message registered. Then Pharaoh moved out quick with TutuoHamic the Chief Astrologer, Hudene the Chief Magician and Polohamic the Chief Priest following.

Soldiers, lots of Soldiers, all bare chested but for a wide leather sling that hung over one shoulder front and back to loop around the hilt of a short metal sword just below the opposite shoulder. Cream colored scarf's rapped over their head hung down in the rear enough to cover their neck with matching waist kilts that reached almost to the knees and leather flats on their feet that tied up around the foot and ankle. All the soldiers stopped their commotion and knelt to one knee as Pharaoh approached. Tiche No, Captain of the Royal Guard was at his Lord's side. Pharaoh saw a small man lay limp and bent over one of the camels, red stains clearly soaked about his rich tunic. One of the engineers, Pharaoh could tell, dead. "SOMEONE REPORT!" He demanded.

Zaph'nathpaane'ah dropped smoothly off a high camel and took one step forward toward Pharaoh before dropping to one knee and bowing his head and raising out his arms, palms up in a graceful supplicant position. "My Lord and Patron," he said before lifting his eyes to Pharaohs. "This man was Kupshoe, one of your most gifted engineers, he road ahead of our band to represent us for this morning's meeting till we could arrive. We caught up to him waylaid by wicked thieves, he was already dead to this world when we came upon him." Zaph waited another moment for the sound of his words to fully settle then rose, as he did the soldiers also rose and turned back to their former commotion.   One young soldier with a yellow turban denoting his rank immediately stepped out of the group and forward to Tiche's far side, "Captain, we came upon the dead man even as the Governor's caravan was in the far distance, it was as he said. We dare not search out the thieves but decided to escort the Governor." Tiche nodded; Pharaoh took in the whole of the matter before him then returned into his tent. He could hear Tiche No taking charge of the dead body and dispatching scouts to return to the site of yet another murder of one of his servants. Tiche needs no direction, Pharaoh thought as he entered his tent.

The four Chief Counselors entered Pharaoh's tent and took seats about the table. All was silent for a moment then Pharaoh spoke, "Zaph, I am sorry about the engineer Kupshoe, the third royal servant this month. Nevertheless YOU were ordered to be here for this meeting and YOU were not here. This your Pharaoh can not excuse." Zaph bowed his head till his forehead touched the table. The others watched. Pharaoh continued, "You will not disobey again at pain of five lashes and other five in remembrance of this meeting. Pharaoh hath spoken." Zaph responded with calm sincerity, "I have offended the servant of God forgive my offence, ten lashes will be a fair mercy my Lord but I shall not offend thee again." Pharaoh nodded in agreement, "What news have you of the above ground silo design?" Zaph bowed his head again touching the table with his forehead then stood, "Good news my Lord, the engineers have invented a solution where there was none. May I summon two into Pharaoh Tent that accompanied me here to my Lord?" Pharaoh nodded and Zaph stood and gestured to the doorway as the others quietly looked on. "Lord Pharaoh, may I present two of thy ingenious servants Ralph'Iaro and Polo." Two men entered the tent looking a bit uncomfortable and every bit the number counters, men whom understand the mystery of mathematics. Pharaoh, for his part, simply gazed at the men, the other three Lords of empire copied their Pharaoh's expression leaving the two men feeling visibly awkward and glancing at Zaph for direction. Zaph smiled at them reassuringly, "Please friends, set out your charts here on the table and explain your idea to Pharaoh."

"AH AM," Ralph cleared his throat and began hesitantly. "Mighty Pharaoh and Lords of the Court, the engineering staff has searched for a solution. Inspirited by your words and deeds Mighty Pharaoh, we proceeded day and night knowing that nothing is impossible." Pharaoh nodded at the compliment and Ralph began to feel self confidence returning, "We have designed an enormous silo that rest above the ground, you will see the design is different from anything we have ever constructed before but we have determined that it will work. Also the design is not so different from smaller constructs already used by our stone masons and other crafters." As Ralph spoke, Polo began removing scrolls from his leather carry bag and unrolling them on the table before them.

Pharaoh leaned forward, with his Lords to pear at the simple design. It was two elongated blocks, one larger than the other like a giant step, against the taller step leaned a long support ramp. A measurement line from top of the tallest block and another from well below the blocks bisected some distance away at a point level with the bottom of the blocks forming a perfect triangle.   "With your permission gentleman," Ralph said, "We call these blocks rectangles, the top and bottom plains are equal squares and the side faces are equal lengths but longer then the top and bottom, a square that has been stretched upward. The primary rectangle is a tower. The shorter secondary rectangle is set next to the primary for mutual stability and these dual towers are the Pharaoh's Corn Silos." Ralph looked about to see that everyone was following him.   "The tower is special, first it has the required space needed to properly store most of the corn needed, 222 feet high and 33 by 22 feet in width. It is also designed to be sectioned off, we fill lower levels and seal each level with granite slabs to help preserve the corn and simply work our way up to the top," he smiled in self satisfaction.   Polo continued for Ralph, "Yes, yes, but our real innovation is the tower itself. We have designed it top heavy. Large stone blocks can be lowered from the top and even levered out to help with construction of the surrounding structure. The tower also supports the high side of the construction ramp, as you see here; the line descends from the tower top a proper 26 degree slope."   As Polo took a breath, Ralph jumped in, "The tower and attached ramp is multipurpose, a crane and a silo.   Pharaoh raised both hands, "Wait a minute." He studied the top parchment, then lifted to the second and inhaled sharply. "You propose one single silo, a great tower that will not fall over", Pharaoh said slowly, "large enough to hold seven years worth of corn, a single silo with seven sections, instead of seven separate silos?" He paused, "this is fantastic, this has possibility and it has style."

Pharaoh smiled at the two engineers, "Go on, please show us the details." Ralph continued head now held high, "Around it we build a large pyramid mountain that will maintain the cool temperature required to store Pharaoh's corn." Everyone stared in silence for several minutes.   Finally Tutuo looked up from the parchment, "seven years worth of corn in one single silo?"   Polo nodded yes, "it would actually be quicker to build with this design then several smaller pyramid silos." The Chief Priest broke the next silence by lifting the top parchment to reveal the other that had caused his Pharaoh to suddenly inhale. It had the same diagram as the top parchment but with added measurement lines and the outline of an enormous step pyramid surrounding the tower, very big. The Lords all stared in amassment, good idea or no, it was clearly what their Pharaoh was looking for, it was something great. Under was another parchment listing several stone blocks by size, type and the number of each required for a foundation, tower structure, design and ramp. By each were math equations.

"How is the corn to be dropped into the silo?"   Ralph jumped ahead of Polo this time, "This was the easy part, my Lord, you can see on the next parchment," he lifted the third to reveal the forth. "We have designed a series of load shafts to enter the silo from outside the pyramid, as you can see here, these load shafts are set at a forty degree angle into work rooms set atop each tower where the corn can be sifted and raked into the silo storage area below."   Polo now leaned forward and pointed, "These shafts are easily fabricated and positioned in the center of the open North and South sides. The shafts will have to be level for six feet out of each room to maintain the tower stability then the proper slope can be secured by the surrounding structure. It looks a bit complicated at first glance but really quite simply, everything is built outward from the tower at set angles, once the tower and ramp are completed, everything else is simply attached to it."   Ralph interjected, "The craftsmen will be building something brand new but with the same techniques they are currently familiar with."

Tutuo followed the lower line from the bisection point downward to an underground chamber, "I am guessing this is for the corn that must be collected until the tower can be completed?"   "Yes Lord Tutuo," Ralph responded. "The tower itself can be completed in a couple months, about the same time as the basement." Pharaoh was now comparing the parchments side by side and detail by detail. "The surrounding pyramid will by necessity be, well, enormous! No doubt it will be the largest manmade building in the whole world." Pharaoh finally said, partly to himself, "Yes, yes, yes, I approve."

Governor Zaph watched his Pharaoh's facial expression as he was absorbing all the information, after all Zaph knew that whatever plan Pharaoh decided to pursue, it would be his tasked to see it through to completion. His own head rested solely on the success of the food storage program. His own life and death were one with the prophecy of the seven year famine. Zaph, also called Joseph, had spent the past several years in Pharaoh's dungeons by a noble woman's false accusation. While in prison he had befriended Pharaoh's Chief Butler during his short stay and wonders of wonders, the Butler had remembered him and made recommendation for him before Pharaoh. Hmmm, Zaph thought, once again, Who you know is more important than What you know; but What you know and what people think you know can determine Who you know. The mystery of the circle is revealed in all things.

He glanced across the tent to where young Khufu sat. The Prince was watching him, Zaph smiled acknowledgement before looking back to the business at hand. The young Prince is curious about me, a Hebrew, maybe the only one he has ever seen, once a slave, now his father's newest Chief Governor, only God knows how many have come and gone before me. Some gamble bets against how long I will survive this posting. Zaph saw the other Lords discussing the quarry locations and the material logistics to the Giza Plateau. Whatever Pharaoh decides I must live and breathe it, motivating, cheering, solving the day by day problems and most of all sabotaging any saboteurs. The murder of Kupshoe was not coincidence. Zaph studied each of his fellow Lords. Two weeks into my job and seven hard, dangerous years to go. Very Dangerous!

Pharaoh stood to his feet and waved a hand for silence, "BUTLER!" he called aloud and the Chief Butler himself emerged into Pharaoh's tent with a graceful bow. "Take note Butler and forward to the Recorder. These two servants, Ralph'laro and Polo are honored by Pharaoh, King of Egypt, and shall receive each a Gold Chain of State and land here in the village of Cairo for which to build their own estate even as they manage Pharaoh's Giza Project." The two men fell to their faces and now rose with the broad grins of children that just found a pottery jar full of candies. "The entire remaining engineering staff shall each be given a house in Cairo and daily provisional increase and ordered to begin work immediately." Butler nodded that every word was memorized and ready to be acted upon. "Also," Pharaoh continued, "Have the head remove from that 'former' Chief Engineer." The broad grins of Ralph and Polo disappeared. Pharaoh continued, "Send for General Abdu'ra and tell him the army is to report here and make preparations to assist in all labors. Proclaim in all the cities of Egypt that Pharaoh's Giza Project needs skilled men and women and beast and each shall receive his hire according to the will of Governor Zaph'nathpaane'ah. Pharaoh hath spoken." Again Butler nodded and confirmed aloud, "Pharaoh hath spoken." Pharaoh was very pleased, his Red Pyramid will be only a shadow to this marvel.

Then his Butler glancing to the diagrams on the table said, "And what, Mighty Pharaoh, shall this pyramid be called?" Pharaoh followed his glance to the diagrams then looked out the tent door, visualizing the enormous monument behind his Sphinx towering upward into the heavens with perfect summitry and style. The thought came to him unbidden, "The Great Pyramid, Pharaoh hath spoken. It shall be known for all time as THE GREAT PYRAMID."

Part Two = REBELS IN THE CAMP

[One year into the Seven of Plenty]   Hatem leaned back into the dark shadows and watched as TutuoHamic, Chief Astrologer of Egypt and Lord Counselor to Pharaoh, lighted off his camel and looked in Hatem's direction. Suddenly two cloaked men passed by his concealment and approached Tutuo.

Finally something profitable to report, Hatem thought, it has been nearly one full year since that damn Giza Project began and since Governor Zaph contracted him to spy on one Lord Tutuo. There has always been money to make on the intrigue of great men, but he liked this Governor whose star was rising in Egypt.

Hatem peered closely, these two men that approached Tutuo in the dark were rouges; theft, murder, oh he has seen these type before. Fortunately he was just close enough to make out their conversation,   "How much do they want for the job?" Tutuo was asking, immediately upon seeing the two approach.
So, Hatem thought, Lord Tutuo knows them well, no need for introductions or even casual pleasantries.   "The Pharaoh is well protected and his servants loyal to a fault, they say it will have to be an assassination of opportunity. Maybe tomorrow, maybe next week."   In the shadow Hatem held his breath. "They have been hired to his royal barge so they will be very close to Pharaoh when he travels down river." The one rouge was saying, "Land is what they want, land when the deed is done and gold now."   Tutuo nodded understanding, "They have no idea which Lord buys their services?"   "None, only that a senior Lord of the Court pays in land and gold."   Tutuo nodded again, "Good, give them two bags gold coin and remind them you watch from a distance. Remind them Pharaoh has betrayed the Egyptian people. Also tell them I shall betray them to Pharaoh two weeks from this day if the job is not done."   This time the two rouges bowed slightly then turned back toward Hatem's position. He leaned forward ever so slightly to see their faces, but the movement was perceptible. One of the rouges suddenly shifted his eyes into the shadow ahead. Hatem froze stiff and held his breath.   "HO THERE, STEP FORWARD FOR A COIN," the Rouge suddenly called aloud.

Tutuo turn back in the saddle he had just reined to see his two rouges suddenly leap forward toward a figure crouched in a shadow. The figure darted fast, across the ally and over a short fence and his rouges pursued just as fast. "A DAMN SPY!" Tutuo turned the camel hard and galloped back down the street to cut off the chase. Two more camel riders farther down the road saw their Master suddenly turn his mount and flee in the opposite direction and they came up the street at a gallop to his assistance.

Hatem ran hard. He was first delighted to see his persistence following Tutuo would pay off big time, now he feared the payoff was going to be blood instead of coin, his blood. Over two short fences, across two alleys, around a corner then turned suddenly long knife in hand. The sound of pursuit stopped suddenly back around the corner, he listened hard suppressing his own breathing. One person only, where was the second rouge. Then a sharp pain, Hatem looked down and saw the end of a blade protruding through his chest and heart from the back. Blood was spilling out around the blades point. Turn and fight he thought; Scream out he thought; Breath he thought. The darkness increased and then, he thought no more.

The next morning, Zaph was straining his neck high inside the Great Pyramid tower to see where Khufu pointed. "Here, do you see. I helped set all these blocks over here. It was very hard work, let me tell you." Zaph nodded, "Very good work Prince, I think it may be the best set section of the whole tower." Khufu, Prince of Egypt, eldest of the Queen Mother but youngest son of Pharaoh's many lesser wives, was climbing a pole ladder to point out his cartush name written near the top corner of the center tower just below the huge stone slabs that formed the upper most peeked ceiling. "Do you see Uncle Zaph, right up there. These men assure me it will be covered over with rose granite so that construction overlord Heman will not know. You will not tell him, you will not, he is extremely possessive of every measurement and movement. You would think he plans to entomb himself here when the famine is over."

Zaph listened to the Princeling while trying to stay out of the way of busy workmen. He himself had much to do but fostering a good relationship with the Pharaoh-In-Waiting was on that list. He had just returned from inspection of the first full harvest season along all the Nile cities of Egypt concerning local food programs. Each one had to be organized differently based on each town's resources and temperament toward Pharaoh's decree. Managing receipt and delivery of a fifth part of all corn output was much less of a problem. Pharaoh was paying for the delivery cost.

"LORD KHUFU!" Zaph shouted above the noise of nearby work crews, "We must leave now to catch the early barge back down to Memphis. Your Father ordered us to meet with him. Come now, its ten lashes for your poor Uncle if he is not on time for a meeting with Pharaoh." He watched as Khufu placed each foot to the outside of the ladder post and slid down far too fast, making Zaph wince. If the Prince broke a leg or worse while under my watch it could be more than ten lashes, it might be an eye for an eye. "Your highness," Zaph whispered to Khufu as the two of them rushed down the dark corridor that lead to the Great Pyramid's exit. "I noticed some of those stone masons were Thebeians, you should be wary working with them, you know they consider themselves a subkingdom rather than fully part of your father's rule. Such men of Thebes could be a danger to you. There lords are image worshipping Greeshens and made me very uncomfortable when I was there. I fear rebellion from them in the future." "Nonsense, they are my servants." Khufu responded matter of fact. "Besides you are a Hebrew, should I fear treason from you?" Zaph stopped suddenly at that comment and dropped to one knee, head bowed. Khufu pulled himself up short, "Rise and run with me friend Joseph, I meant nothing by such words. You must forgive my loose tongue, I am not the Pharaoh of Egypt, not for many years."

Tiche No entered into the great throne room of Memphis, "LORD PHARAOH!" He shouted in a strong soldier's voice, "The honorable TutuoHamic Chief Astrologer to the Family Royal!" Pharaoh turned from his lovely wife and waved a beckoning hand. Tutuo, having seen the wave strode inside even as Tiche No was turning back to him.

The Throne room walls were built of large stone blocks with a line of columns around the inside perimeter that supported the high ceiling about six foot above the walls allowing natural light and soft breeze wash over the ivory throne. The great throne sat on a wide platform that filled the far end of the great hall, the platform was only one big step up from the floor of the hall and gave plenty of room for Pharaoh to walk about or set seats for his Queen, chamber wives or children. His Pharaoh was standing now on the platform making a comment to Queen Hetephis. She responds with a silent laugh placing her hand delicately on her husband's arm. Pharaoh turns toward him with a smile, "My friend Tutuo what have you this morning?" Tutuo bowed low then lifted himself high. Stepping onto the platform he reached into his bright blue tunic and his hand brushed the ivory handle of his blade and he smile broadly. "This, my Lord." He reached past the blade and pulled out the papyrus roll and presented it into Pharaoh's hand. "My Lady," Tutuo said with another bow. She stretched forth her hand to him with all the grace of a polished Queen. She would be spared, he thought, such a woman of Egypt must survive the blood coming on her house.

"TutuoHamic," she said in that sweet feminine voice that made light music of the words, "you are always about the people's business from early morning to late evening and my people are grateful to you." Pharaoh examined the papyrus. "You are kind as you are lovely my Queen," Tutuo said smoothly with the barest hint of pride, "I only desire to see the birthright of Ham continue through your family as the true heirs of our fathers. If we are The People, we must prove it again each and every day." The Queen withdrew her hand, "Always so serious dear Tutuo, but God has made one for this and another for that." Her bright large eyes flashed regal confidence. "Good day to you; husband I shall take my leave for we girls have much planned for today." Bowing slightly to Pharaoh she turned away but Pharaoh looked up again and caught her hand and gentle raised it to his lips. Their eyes meet in mutual unspoken words of love, then she departed, every bit the polished ebony Queen.

Pharaoh turned to Tutuo, "Walk with me Counselor." The two strolled down the length of the Throne Hall, pass the guards and down the broad corridor of rounded pillars that lead to the Common Hall and out into the bright sun light.

The two men discussed the production levels at the various quarries, they were back up to full capacity, turning out nearly seven blocks per hour, per site. This put as many as three hundred stone blocks a day on route to the Giza Plateau. His cousin Heman overseeing the actual construction site would be pleased. "Now before I take my leave of you loyal Tutuo," Pharaoh said. "Tell me what do you read in the stars, tell me what signs do your astrologers observe?" As he continued his lackadaisical stroll across the palace courtyard. Some of the royal children ran back and forth yelling in play with each other. Tutuo still strolled alongside his King and thought to himself, separating truth and lies.

Finally he responded as Chief Astrologer, "My Glorious King, your star will be crossed by a slow moving comet, at least from our viewing perspective. Surely it is a sign of a portentous event. Heaven confirms it." Tutuo continued, "Maybe it signals the words of young Joseph, ah, Zaph'nathpaane'ah." Tutuo enjoyed making the small mishap. Zaph was a criminal proficient in supervising Pharaoh's dungeons but not qualified to supervise his Kingdom, not even of proper birth. "Did he not say seven years of plenty." Pharaoh nodded. "I admire the talents of this newest Governor Zaph, very hard working too." Pharaoh nodded again. "But please indulge me Rightful Lord of all men, I must again counsel thee to beware of promoting other races within your kingdom, we are their superiors. In time our younger brothers may cast us down Ra forbid." Pharaoh smiled, "I doubt any black man could be cast down for long, still your words on this matter begin to disappoint me. Pharaoh is King and all men may serve him as God wills them to." The two were drawing nearer the river Nile that channeled off from the main to lap the edge of the palace grounds. A royal boat waited on dock with a ready crew. Tutuo realized Pharaoh was purposely making his way to the boat, likely going down river from Memphis to the Giza Plateau for inspection of the Great Pyramid Project. He was going to meet with that Joseph, Blasted winds. "Wise Lord, your understanding is perfect; by the way my cousin Galo'Ralao has developed a new star gazing scope that I dearly wish for you to see." This time Pharaoh smiled broadly, "I shall my dear Counselor, I shall." And with that Pharaoh turned directly to the dock and the waiting boat. Tutuo watched for only a moment, he saw the oarsmen standing ready before turning his own way.

The luxury Liner pushed off from the docks and caught the current. The oarsmen began a slow chant that blended with the sounds of water against the haul guiding the twenty oars to move in perfect unison. Oars man was considered a good job among the lower classes, especially on a royal ship and these men took pride in their skill. Pharaoh enter the boat house and took a seat at the head of his table. Governor Zaph, his father in law who was the Priest of On and Polohamic the Chief Priest stood for their King then sat back down.

Pharaoh said, "I trust you have been briefed by Tiche No, that the murdered engineer Kupshoe was branded like the others." Each man nodded in acknowledgement. Over the past couple years employees of Pharaoh and even the occasional royal cousin had turn up murdered, each one bearing a mark across the belly. The symbol of a crow with the torso and legs of a man. In the past few months the murders had dramatically increased.

Polohamic folded his hands and rested them atop his own belly, "Mighty Pharaoh, idol worship has spread across the cities of our brethren in Canaan and the cities of our cousins in Babylonia. Now it spreads here among our people. Not only among our peasants but secretly among the nobility. It targets you and your Great House, there is no doubt of it, the agenda behind this enhanced religion is to overthrow your government, your family and establish a new Dynasty." Pharaoh considered a long moment, "Can we introduce idols of our own for the people to purchase, maybe the likeness of minor gods for each city and town?" Now it was Polohamics turn to consider a long moment, "We could, but RA has no likeness. I fear the people will soon declare these demigods to be gods and the faith of Noe and Ham will fade away. Besides the killings will continue because the movement is only using religion to take the throne." The priest of On asked, "How do they expect to claim a throne held by birthright and lineage, have they secretly recruited one of your brothers or uncles? Surely they do not believe the people will accept a Common Pharaoh?" The Chief Priest turned his heft in the chair, "The idols are personal, gods in their own image and after their own imaginations, in time they will accept a common Pharaoh if he or even she is chosen by their common gods. We have seen it already in the north among the Canaanite tribes and the Greeshan clans."

"The Days Of The Birthright Kings Are Coming To An End In The World Of Men. The Days Of Cunning And Muscle And Of Demy-God Kings Has Already Begun."

At this Pharaoh made up his mind, "We shall allow more of the idols, archangels with the bodies of men and the faces of animals such as are described by the ancients. Tell their stories to the people. Sell their images, for God has given them an image. If we cannot stop the tied then we shall direct its flow. None should sacrifice unto them, these demigods shall have no alters or temples in the land of Egypt in which they minister. In this way the people shall have their images but not so quickly forget RA who sees all." He sighed aloud, "Ah, Pharaoh hath spoken." Polohamic bowed his head, "Yes. Pharaoh hath spoken. For good or ill, none yet know." Zaph sat respectfully quite as if contemplating some series of future events.

Pharaoh looked at Zaph, "You have enemies within my court, surely you know this already." Zaph nodded in acknowledgement and watched his Pharaoh's face completely, taking in every nuance reflected by his eyes and mouth and brow and creases of the skin. He learned by long years as a slave to observe the details of the face when a man spoke and when a man listened. Thoughts and intentions were revealed there, not in simple words but in pictures. The face presented a near endless series of pictures and each picture was worth a thousand words. Pharaoh continued, "You also have many friends and admirers throughout the land, good reports reach my ears from many of my City Lords. They praise your hard word and skills as a Governor. You have also become somewhat of a folk hero to the peasants. The man that rose from slavery and prison to rule over all Egypt." Pharaoh smiled. "I think men shall tell stories of you long after I am forgotten." Zaph smiled with his Pharaoh, "Then may I be remembered as Imanhotep, loyal and trust worthy, the servant of God and of Pharaoh." "I decree it so." Pharaoh responded. "But here and now, I need you to earn that reputation. I face enemies of my own, murders and thieves that seek my life and hope to bring down my families Dynasty. Surely you already know the great dangers that face Egypt." Zaph harden his face to match the gravity of his Pharaoh's words. He saw from Pharaoh's face that he was becoming increasingly troubled, the dangers to his nation were very real. He had been traveling back and forth across upper and lower Egypt for the past two years now. Many rumors had reached his ears, numerous unsolved murders of Pharaoh's functionaries, even threats from wild tribes along the borders. The bulk of the army stationed at the Giza plateau for so long had begun emboldening highwaymen and the rebellious.

"Great Pharaoh," Zaph began. "Do not be distracted from your purpose or all Egypt, I tell you, all Egypt shall parish in the coming famine. Neither man or beast shall survive. Remember your own counsel Mighty Father, King of Memphis, less than six years and all your enemies will be astonished to see the desolation sweep across the land. Their stomachs will speak and their own servants murmur against them for bread. Only Pharaoh will be prepared. He whom Pharaoh feeds will live and he whom Pharaoh does not feed will die."

Pharaoh nodded, "Yes, yes I know. Shall my house survive six more years? That is the concern." He sighed, "The harvest are so plenty that corn prices have fallen through the floor, the people bring a fifth of the corn without complaint and we have laborers a plenty on the Giza project. That is something. Your right once again my good counselor, patients is the path I must keep to." "But tell me mighty Joseph; tell me what you have seen in that cup of divination? God speaks no more to me in dreams beyond the two He has already given. I have obeyed fully and in accordance to thy counsel, yet my enemies multiply round about. What have you seen regarding your Pharaoh?"

Zaph rose from his seat and knelt reverently before Pharaoh, "You have honored me and do honor me yet again. To serve you and your Great House has been my privilege this past year." Zaph rose to stand before the regal Pharaoh, as was his habit, Zaph moved his left arm about as he spoke. "As you said, I was a prisoner in Pharaoh's dungeon for several years, I served my God with good deeds toward my fellows and obeyed Pharaoh's lesser servants in all things. Thou O Pharaoh called upon me in the day appointed and required the interpretation of the dreams. And thou O Pharaoh made me Governor in Egypt. Since, I have worked day and night, more than any of thy other servants for thy success and ultimate victory over thy enemies."

"Yet I do not see in my divination your success, rather I see thy son. Thy son Khuf'Ruham, I have seen him standing on both the head and neck of all thy enemies, indeed on all of Egypt. Khufu appears as a thick cedar whose branches reach out over Canaan and Babylonia and even beyond the isles of Greesha." I cannot see clearly but as through a glass darkly; why I cannot see you, does it not trouble me with sorrows? Still I seek thy face, yet it is hidden from me." Casting his eyes to the floor, Zaph paused.

Pharaoh watched him keenly, the intelligence bright in his eyes. Then looking away, "I wonder at Tutuo's comet that will soon cross my star." Pharaoh seemed to be lost in thought, connecting unseen dots. He murmured, "Tutuo's Comet, now that I consider, how sadly ironic." "Lord?" Zaph said. Pharaoh sighed. Refocusing on his Counselor, "Seek no more for that which cannot be found, it is enough grace that my House and my people continue." With that he turned and walked out onto the deck, dismissing any further conversation.

THE KING IS DEAD - LONG LIVE THE KING

The attack was sudden and brutal. Khufu turned back from Zaph. "Father," he called out across the ship's deck. His father turned his head, their eyes met, a great Pharaoh and his young son. The trust, the mutual admiration, even love passed in that moment from one pair of eyes to the other. Then Khufu's eyes drifted slightly down and left of his Pharaoh's gaze by some movement that should not have been there. Of all things, a rower seemed to have stepped away from his oar and unbelievable toward his Pharaoh from behind., but no that was not permitted. Then as swift as a lightning bolt in a desert storm, the glimmer of metal, a knife swung around Pharaohs neck and pulled back deep. Khufu was frozen in place his mind recording the event but not comprehending. He locked eyes again with his father and saw in the twinkle Pharaoh's compassion for him, his questioning look of what Khufu had wanted, then awareness of trouble, and finally painful realization of what was happening to him. All in a sudden and brutal moment, a series of living twinkles within the eyes, it was over.

His Father just crumpled to the deck. Bright red blood flowing down the front of his fine clothes, bleeding into the bleached white, soft greens, pure golds and then across the polished wood planking all about him. Khufu was aware now of what was happening. Shock! Some distant part of his brain registered, but no reason or logic nor possible humanity would register; his body frozen in place.

From beside him, a blur of Zaph darted by in full run toward the murderer, a long dagger appearing in his hand. Zaph was shouting, "NOOOOOOO!" He seemed to move like a desert genie enraged. Still dumfounded, Khufu watched as another oarsman stepped out of place and raise a short dagger. It was all so fast yet slow motioned at the same time. This man was looking at him, Khufu's eyes met his even as they had met his Fathers' only moments ago, but here he saw hatred, a murderous intention and determination. Khufu only stared at the man as he was preparing to through his blade directly at him. Detached, Khufu just stared at him in wonder bewilderment. Zaph must have detected the hostel movement from his peripheral vision, for in that instant he turned his body in mid stride and struck the assassin against the side of his face with the back of his fist. The man reeled and brought the knife down instead slashing through Zaph's arm. Blood splattered even as Zaph fell back swinging his other hand with the blade around, slashing at the assassins face but missing by inches. Zaph lost his footing, slipping backwards to the deck of the ship only feet away from the Pharaoh' body.

Suddenly a short spear whipped through the air with such force, passing fully through the second assassin. This time Khufu saw the twinkle of astonishment pass in the oarsman's eyes then it was his turn to crumple down to the deck. A bellowing war cry came from Khufu's right as Tiche No, who had obviously thrown the spear charged into view, sword now drawn. The first assassin saw him coming and his fellow fall and turned and leapt over the side of the boat into the hard current of the Nile River. Two other oarsman that had been working between the assassins glanced at the dead Pharaoh and considered their relative position also leaped into the water and began to swim furiously away. Tiche No reached his Pharaoh's body and swung his sword around in a great ark seeking out another assassin, finding none, he screamed in vengeful rage, "DAMN YOU TO HELL" then leapt into the river in obvious pursuit of the murderer. The boat drifted toward the near shore as everyone on board stood transfixed.

Tiche's spearmen protectively surrounded Khufu. Zaph had gotten to his knees and was now bent over Pharaoh's body. Everyone heard him crying, sobbing shamelessly loud and beating his fist against the blood soaked planks of the deck. "How Have The Mighty Fallen, O God! How Have The Wicked Prevailed, O God! O MY GOD!" he screamed. Then Khufu finally collapsed, tears flowing down his face, his spirit broken and he wailed a terrible, evil sound.

When the Royal ship finally pulled up to the docks along the Giza Plateau; five hundred soldiers stood in ranks at attention, eyes cast downward. Khufu stepped along the gang plank to the rocky limestone shore. On the near plateau stood an enormous step pyramid still under construction. A square tower rose up through its center and long ropes reached out from it to teams of men and beast working about the different levels under construction. The pyramids base was enormous. Stone blocks stood in lines from its base and stretched out for what seemed miles. Groups of workmen could be seen moving about like well organized ants before their mound.

Zaph'nathpaane'ah the Governor stepped off behind him and behind them the spearmen of the Royal Guard. Around Khufu's neck was the heavy gold chain of State which bore the round medallion of RA with the Cartush symbols of Horus and Osiris working in the center surrounded by two pyramids that formed the mysterious hexagram star. Zaph watched, he knew time was of the essence. Khufu was barely a teenager, but he must secure the throne quickly before an older brother or cousin saw opportunity to usurp the Prince Royal. Young Khufu had visibly changed during the short distance they traveled since the attack less than an hour ago. Khufu had hardened as if ten hard years had passed, a cruelness that Zaph feared would never abate appeared in his words. The work on the Great Pyramid would be stopped for the forty days of mourning and embalming of the Great Pharaoh. He would have to reorganize all the work crews again and reestablish the lost momentum. I must walk a delicate edge, guiding the boy true without being seen as a usurper myself. Zaph thought, and the rebels in the camp would have to be discovered.

Zaph motioned for General Abdu'ra of the Army to approach him. "Dispatch an hundred men to Memphis with all speed." He said, "Command them to announce along the way and about the city and lastly before the Queen Mother the words you hear now, namely that Pharaoh is slain by rebels and Khufu reigns in Egypt! Also the army marches with him and the sacred body of his father back to the Capitol."   The General regarded him a few moments, weighing the man now behind the Throne. "So it is all true." He paused again. "I shall cast in my lot." He finally said, "and march beside our new Pharaoh back to Memphis so all shall know where I stand. I honor his father and so honor the son."   "Then go quickly General before our enemies can take counsel."

The Faithful Butler stepped around them and proclaimed in a loud voice, "Behold Pharaoh Khufu! Long Live the King!" All the soldiers, all the people about bent the knee before him and repeated "Pharaoh Khufu! Long Live the King!" The soldiers repeated again and again, "Pharaoh Khufu! Long Live the King!" As the sound carried up the plateau, workman stopped to see, then fell to their knees and joined the chant. Within a minutes time the whole of Giza was bowed low and chanting. The Eye of Ra high above shined bright upon them. "Pharaoh Khufu! Long live the King!"

Part Three = **BITTER - SWEET**

[One year into the Great Famine]   The troops marched forward, one thousand men in companies of one hundred. Each soldier wore the leather hide sandals that wrapped neatly around the foot and tied around the ankle. The knee length cream colored kilt that belted at the waist, leaving their dark muscular chest bare. The squared off head scarf that set atop the head and hung down in the back. The leather strap around neck and left shoulder that secured each man's metal sword under that arm. The short throwing spear tipped with sharp copper point in one hand and small round hippo-hide shield in the other. These were Egypt's finest; trained, disciplined, full time professional solders. Each man stomped the ground hard with his right foot as they marched, then moved forward in unison to stomp again with the right foot. The action gave the troops a pulsing motion forward, a formidable desert Army. As far as Pharaoh knew, they were the only year around army in the world. Most kingdoms kept a professional guard but armies were seasonal, laborers and lords called to arms temporarily. But not here, this was a National Army, one thousand strong men marshaled by the ten lords of Egypt, fed and housed by Pharaoh's government. Above them flew the long flowing banners of the ten provinces and famous cartushes of the great families. Drums beat to the march. Dust rose about the ground. The troops were marching up the desert incline onto the huge limestone plateau known as Giza.

Ten strong war wagons each pulled by a yoke of oxen followed the troops. After came a band of sorts. One hundred handsome men and women danced about with tambourines and flutes. They were bare foot and dressed only in colorful grass miniskirts. Their bare skin glimmered with a light sheen of sweat, muscular chest and soft breast turning from side to side with the music. The young women drummed the tambourines in a fine rhythm and from time to time they raddled them high over their heads and sang out in unison. Their male counter parts blew on the flutes as they danced in tune. Together they impressed and entertained onlookers, providing a liberal contrast to the conservative army. They sang to the glories of Egypt, the glories of Pharaoh and of God.

Following was another one hundred, unlike the band these were fully dressed in white robes and tall white feathers weaved into their hair. Each one carried a sweeper broom walking backwards and sweeping the sand smooth. Occasionally reaching down to snatch a loose stone and tossing it low off to the side. From the perspective of the onlookers, these appeared to be constantly bobbing and bowing while leaving the ground as if no one had ever stepped upon it. The object of their adoration followed.

Twenty five strong men on each side walked with a bridge suspended upon their shoulders. Upon the raised platform sat a teenager. He sat on a palm throne that was polished to a translucent shine. He was dressed in rich yellows and greens and bore the small golden shepherd Staff and Thrash of State. He was Pharaoh Khufu! At his feet were woven rugs and feathered pillows. Above his head waved giant plums. And he watched from side to side, his people looking up at him in awe before bowing their heads toward the ground.

Zaph also watched the young King from his spot on an up cropping of the plateau. A mighty Dynasty indeed. The young man had gained a hard reputation since the brutal murder of his father which they had both witnessed only seven years ago. His first order as Pharaoh was the immediate execution of all the oarsmen still aboard the barge and warrants sent out for the murderer that escaped and for the Captain that had perused after him.

Rural families from across Egypt lined both sides of the causeway. Many of the men appeared to be poor farmers from the rural creeks far outside any of the suburbs and migrant workers. Their children ran back and forth continued to play. None appeared starved near death but most were clearly malnourished. The Great Famine had begun one year ago just as Pharaoh had predicted to them. But the severity of this famine was shocking, even to those that were expecting it. The parade of the full Army to the Giza sent a message loud and clear to all that stood by to watch, Pharaoh's corn was securely his own.

As the royal platform passed on up the plateau it was followed by three covered wagons bearing his administrative servants. And finally followed up with fifty or so camel riders, these were serious men, the Palace Guards in orange kilts and turbans charged with security of the Pharaoh and his family.

It was then one of Zaph's own security men approached him, "Your Honor, a peasant man over here insist on speaking to you." Zaph continued to watch the royal precession as it approached but tilted his head to hear the message. "He ask no corn or favor, only to give you a secret message of some importance." Zaph waved his hand, "Bring him." His security man returned, hand on sword with a giant peasant. The man was dirty and worn strong from hard work and hard times, the man knelt to one knee and Zaph was suddenly aware he knew the man, yes, no, it could not be. Seven years had passed, but surely it was. Zaph leaned forward, "Captain Tiche No".

"Speak my friend but make your words quick and true, for no one has seen or heard from you ever since your charge, our beloved Pharaoh was murdered." The former Captain stood up to his full height, "No man has recognized me these past years, since I slew the treacherous murderer aboard the royal ship on that fateful day then dove into the Nile in pursuit of his accomplice." Tiche placed his hand over his heart, "Before RA I perused the Villon to a far shore and followed his track a mile inland when I discovered his body slain from a long dagger still in his back. Two sets of camel tracks made off southward." Zaph raised a hand, "give me the details later, what news now that you reveal yourself and peril both our lives?" "I lived as a migrant worker and beggar about the city till I recognized the camel tracks again, the hoof and gape being the same. This time they lead to the servant quarters of TutuoHamic, Royal Counselor to Pharaoh."

He looked into Zaph's eyes, "after these many years working like a slave in his household and spying, I have discovered the evil plot and have now return to my Pharaoh. I shall accept my judgment." Zaph regarded him, truth was in his features and something else, fierce honor, Nobility. "You shall walk behind me head bowed low when I approach Khufu. Wait for me to present you then approach to his feet and prostate yourself. I must withdraw then for prudence

130

sake and you will live or die upon your words and the will of God. Khufu is a hard Pharaoh, short on mercy. Yet he is still a youth that hears my words and considers them." "I know God speaks through you faithful Joseph and reveals secrets, I was their long ago when you divined Pharaoh's dreams. I shall obey your words now." Said Tiche No.

Zaph waved to his own Butler and confidant, "Gather my men quietly. Disperse them casually around the perimeter of Counselor Tutuo's camp. They are to be casual in demeanor but ready for sudden trouble. Then bring me a sword and follow my lead." Pharaoh's train had ascended the Giza and nearing the walkway that rose up to the entrance door of The Great Pyramid. The Lords of Egypt stood nearby in small administrative camps, their private guards protecting each Lords group and discouraging hungry peasants from approaching.

Pharaoh Khufu offered a smile when he saw his friend approaching. Joseph, Zaph as his father had renamed him was like a father figure since his own had died that dreadful day. The man was a Hebrew of the long ago Abraham, known as the friend of God, as his name suggest. But his experiences as a slave by the hands of his own brethren, unimaginable. Zaph had shared that story with him as a comfort after my great father was buried. These left him with scars but also with graces. Khufu knew though he was young that he had his own scars, and he and Zaph shared many good times. This man Joseph is one of the few Lords of Egypt I fully trust, Khufu thought, but our friendship is a danger to him and to me on the Palm and Ivory Throne.

"Welcome Great Pharaoh to The Great Pyramid of Giza, the greatest wonder in the world. As you can see we have begun filling in the steps and the silo spaces are filled to the overflow." Construction Superintendent Heman said aloud beaming with pride. Beside him stood Ralph and Polo the Chief Engineers. Ralph said, "My Lord Pharaoh what a great pleasure it is to see you with our own eyes, as the Eye of Ra you shine upon us." Polo cut in, "As the Eye of Ra and the strength of Isis."

It was then Zaph approached and the others noticing the Pharaoh's Chief Governor stepped back. Many of Pharaoh's aides had appeared from the wagons and his Palace Guard fanned about. Khufu himself was stepping off the bridge platform with his Queen Mother as it was expertly lowered to the ground. "What news Governor?" Khufu said taking in the crowd and his differing Lords of the realm approaching. "WHAT NEWS INDEED!" Cried Zaph aloud. Pharaoh's eyes darted back to his Governor, curiosity appearing. "The gravest of news since these past seven years has reached my ears this very hour." "Indeed?" Said Khufu. The others falling silent as attention moved to Zaph. "Lord Pharaoh is blessed above all men, for he is the very head of the Egyptian Lion, he is wise beyond his years and careful in weighty matters." Khufu's eyes now narrowed, what is my Governor up to? He thought. "This very hour I have taken into custody a notorious person. His head has been sought by my Lord Pharaoh many years. The man not only lives but has told me in part a fantastic tale of which the hearing has astonished me. So I could bear no more the hearing but commanded him to be brought this very moment before my wise and careful Lord to tell the tale in full!" "For I wonder if Pharaoh stands here among his Lords in mortal danger." Now all was completely still and people to close to Khufu leaned back with a sense that the angel of death had suddenly joined the gathering and waited.

Khufu actually showed his astonishment when Captain Tiche No stepped forward and prostrated himself on the ground before the young King. Whispers moved through the gathered assembly, Palace Guards moved forward unsure to see their old commander, Zaph eased backward, the Lords shifted uncomfortably. Khufu's mode darkened as emotions of that murderous day emerged.

"HE LIES! How Dare He who failed in his duty to protect your father now accuse me!" Shouted TutuoHamic as Captain Tiche No finished his tale still prostrated before Khufu. But the tale had the ring of truth and others leaned away from Tutuo. Palace Guards were agitated, drawing weapons and people were suddenly moving back. Two of Tutuo's guards suddenly broke and dashed back through the people seeking flight but were set upon by Zaph's men already in place. The sight of Zaph's guardsmen grabbing two of their own caused Tutuo's guardsmen to draw blades and Pharaoh's Guard moved to surround their King.

Tutuo hesitated a moment then shouted, "STAND DOWN, STAND DOWN! Mighty and Merciful Pharaoh, These Are To Blame; I have served your father and know nothing of my servant's plo…" His words were cut off as the guilty Rouge next to him suddenly understood the situation and stuck a knife into Tutuo's neck, red blood glimmered in the sun light as it spilt down robes and shoes onto the sand and the Counselor fell silent. This rouge everyone knew to be Tutuo's personal enforcer and confidant. He dropped the knife as orange turbaned Palace Guards moved forward to secure him, others dragged forward the other two men that had tried to flee.

"I have slain your treacherous enemy for you my Pharaoh!" The Rouge shouted as he knelt on one knee before Khufu. "I have slain him for you my Pharaoh, for I was ashamed to discover his shame!" None paid Tutuo any mind as he died.

Pharaoh Khufu had set up court and much blood had already been shed. All of Counselor Tutuo's personal assistants had been summarily executed next to their boss's body, now a small pile of bodies and Khufu had sent solders to bring with all speed Tutuo's wives and children. Only the three rouges remained beaten but well enough alive. Captain Tiche No still lay prostrated on the ground for he dare not lift one eye brow till the matter was settled. He had served many years in the court of Pharaoh and knew well how to survive if it were possible. Zaph watched from a quite distance along with the other Lords of Egypt.

Khufu motioned to a Palace Guard and a foot lopped off one of the rouges that attempted to flee earlier. The man screamed and then a foot lopped off the other rouge caught fleeing, that man screamed. Pharaoh lifted his hand for silence and the two men bit into their own lips to remain silent. For even in agony all hope remained with the young Pharaoh, better missing one foot then one's life. "SPEAK!" boomed Khufu.

The pocked face Rouge still bent on one knee spoke first, "These two men my Pharaoh were the villains that road forth on the camels to do their masters biding,

I have slain their master and I will slay these two retches for thee also." He went as to rise but was prevented by guardsmen. The two held their stumps and spoke at once, "Na my lord, Na. We are sorry rouges for sure and cutpurses but he is a sinner of the first order, an evil man. We rode out many times with our master at night and were told to stand off and keep watch, it was this liar before you that performed our master's will." Tears came as one of them said, "Once I was with them about two weeks before your honored father was assassinated and they were spied on. They pursued the spy through the night streets and killed him, one called Hatem. This man knifed him in the back, a spy whom I had known in time past but knew not whom he worked for now. The man glanced toward the Lords for an instant and Zaph knew the man did know whom Hatem had worked for but evidentially not betray the knowledge. "This evil Rouge said to my master and I heard him, 'only two more weeks', but I knew not what they spoke of till two weeks later your Honored Father was killed. I feared then as I fear now for my very soul. Forgive Me Lord Khufu, Forgive Me." The other spoke rapidly voice strained from the pain of his missing foot, "Rumor in our camp was he is also the one that murdered Kupshoe your engineer in the desert on the way to the Giza Meeting." The other was shaking his head, "Pharaoh we have been poor and dumb servants and were born to such weakness, but we have no part in evil deeds. We only fled because of fear and shame at thy Captain's true words." Tears, shakes, one pissed himself. "Go from my face and never shall I look upon you again. Pharaoh hath spoken."

Khufu stepped back, "GIVE THIS GUILTY ROUGE A SWORD!" A sword was given and he took it in expert hand. "Now climb my Pyramid, climb all the way up to the flat top and wait for my champion to come for you." The sun was full in the sky when the rouge turned to start climbing up. "By the way", Khufu called after him, "If you should win the day then you are free!" The Rouge smiled thinly at his luck, and he began to boldly climb The Great Pyramid of Giza.

After a few moments Pharaoh Khufu looked about and announced, "DOES PHARAOH HAVE A CHAMPION?!" He pointedly looked at his Lords of the Realm, his Engineers and various laborers, then across the crowd of common folk gathered about to see all that had happened, finally at the soldiers. Many made as if they wanted to step forward and others did but glanced at the mammoth building flat topped high above. To win would be glory but to lose would not only be deadly but shame your family, maybe your soul. Still some stood forward.

It was then Captain Tiche No rose up from his prostrated position and stood to his full height before Pharaoh, and Pharaoh smiled upon him. "Are you my champion? Have you not failed so far in your duty? Can you prove you're worth this day?" It was so quite every foot step could be heard of the Rouge as he climbed. "All Egypt watches, the Eye of RA watches, the lesser gods pause and Pharaoh's Champion takes up his sword." A small dust devil blew by. Everyone knew they were witnessing a Great Pharaoh in all his Glory and a once in a life time event. Khufu leaned close to Tiche No's ear, "My father trusted you completely and so do I, now go and slay my father's enemy and mine and deliver thy own soul."

The Champion of Pharaoh was given Khufu's own sword from off his mobile platform, the one with the silver handle topped with a red ruby. Tiche No used it to cut away the slave clothing till he stood before the crowd completely naked in all his masculine glory and raised the sword over his head and let out a war cry! And the people shouted!

The crowd of people; men, women and children, laborers and lords watched as the two men climbed the large stones, one after another, level after level. The Great Pyramid was so huge, yet unfinished. The outer layer and smooth surface would not begin for another year after the step levels were completely filled in. The size so enormous that many thought it should remain as it was, maybe add a small temple to the top rather than a giant cap stone. The sun had passed its zenith and the heat shimmered off the desert sands. The murderous Rouge had just reached the summit and stood on the flat top. He seemed a small figure, far away. People watched in anticipation. Pharaoh Khufu had stepped back onto his platform and watch from the throne, the Queen Mother standing at his side, her hands resting on her son.

Tiche No tried to step up on the summit but each time had to retreat downward a step or two. The Rouge had the high ground and appeared to be taking every advantage. The two moved around the summit, the Rouge keeping the Champion down, not letting him step up to the flat top. The two moved to the far side and were not visible. Many of the young people took off running down the base of the pyramid to see the battle progress. After a few moments the two reemerged on this side. Suddenly Tiche No gripped the summit with both hands and ducked low as a sword swung down at him hard, making a ringing sound against the stone. The same instant Tiche No rolled up on top and kept rolling as the rouge recovered his swing and slashed down repeatedly, each time sending an echoing ring down to the onlookers below. He was quick and deadly and clearly trying to finish his opponent as soon as possible without any fan fair. Tiche No rolled three times then stopped on his back sword ready for the vicious swing of his enemy. The two swords glimmered the sunlight and rang out as they met. The Rouge twisted and tried to slide his sword down Tiche's blade for a wounding but Tiche No properly twisted his own blade to prevent such a move and brought his legs around to kick the Rouge's leg. He missed but the step back was enough for Tiche No to gain his footing on top The Great Pyramid.

The Rouge charged the older man, his blade swinging back and forth with speed and firm control. Clearly he meant to end the conflict immediately. Khufu's champion had fought many battles in his day against the Thebien rebellion, against raiders from Nubia, Canaan and even Arabia before taking post as Captain of the Royal Guard. Though older now, the last seven years he has been living a hard life as common labor in several wealthy Houses always keeping his head low and eyes open. Till his careful investigating led him to the House of Tutuo and this filthy Rouge. Tiche was not driven back off the top but kept stepping sideways and forward while parrying the vicious blows. Parry, sideways and forward. Parry, sideways and forward. The rouges blows began to slacken, he was having to constantly turn himself and was growing wary of his opponent. The people below did not see Tiche No smile, but Khufu knew that he must have smiled broadly. His Champion had finally taken the summit and fended back the initial attack. Now he was taking control of the contest. Khufu looked across to Zaph, he watched him a moment unobserved. He had learned so much from him since his father had promoted Zaph from prison to a Governorship. He trust him as a friend and father figure. He looked toward each of his Lords in turn, most were a good lot appointed by his father, a few needed replacing because of old age or personality. But this day's battle would secure his personal safety and popularity against the lean days ahead. After this day none would dare oppose Pharaoh Khufu with the famous Captain Tiche No at his side.

The Rouge was just a rouge, uncommonly cruel and deadly but no mean soldier with endurance for the battle. He swung long and Captain Tiche leaned away then swung a round house punch with his other hand catching him on the chin. The Rouge seemed to freeze in place for a moment, jarred by the blow. But Captain Tiche No showed no mercy where no mercy was given. He followed through with his sword arm. The people gave a collective gasp as the Rouges body suddenly collapse and his head bounced up of the top.

Everyone watched as it fell and rolled then bounced of the stone level below the summit where Khufu's Champion stood a tiny figure triumphant, naked expect for a red sword and sweat reflecting the hot sun. The Rouge's head gained speed as it bounced down from stone to stone, level by level till it reached the base of The Great Pyramid of Giza.

KHUFU'S GOLD

Together they walked beneath the massive trussed stones set above the large doorway inside the pyramid silo. Khufu and Joseph side by side and down the passageway till they reached the corridor upwards. They climbed the corridor up through the great pyramids interior, up through the grand gallery till they reached the top most step. There they passed across the antechamber, bending low to avoid the stone suspended to close off the upper chamber. The two entered the large chamber as their foot falls echoed around the bare walls and up to the peaked ceiling far above. "Do you suppose my name is still on the top most section of wall up their?" Khufu asked. "I suppose it is." Joseph answered. Khufu looked up into the darkness above, "It seems so long ago, we were here together, I was a child playing at helping the workmen, you my mentor and friend, my dad was Pharaoh and the world was…" Khufu cut off, "Well it just seems so long ago." All was silent, the two finally walked over to the edge of the silo opening and peered down. "Khufu's Gold." Joseph said pointing to the mound of corn cornels almost level with the floor. "This is seven years worth of corn, enough to feed a whole nation and we haven't even touched it yet. You should sell it, Egyptian and Canaanite alike will pay this year and the next. You should sell it till you are the richest man in the world. Your father's idea." Khufu nodded, "Yes, the people are cruel and unfaithful, they shall pay and they will learn that I am master of Egypt. GodRa has chosen me and my family, we shall feed them and save Egypt from destruction and we shall use their gold and jewels and precious things to make the world a better place." Joseph bowed, "As you wish my Lord Pharaoh. As you wish."

As the two exited The Great Pyramid onto the wide patio suspended twenty feet above the ground on the north side with its long ramp sloping its way down and bending toward the Nile. A great crowd of people had gathered about on both sides. Many Egyptians wanted to see their young Pharaoh and his court, but from a safe distance. The severity of the famine was bringing more and more people each day. Waiting just outside the great doorway with spear in hand, tall and proud was Tich No, once again Captain of the Royal Guard. Also Polohamic, the sizable Chief Priest and beside him the Priest of On stood speaking to Hudene the Chief Magician. The Chief Engineers Ralph and Polo were smiling. The Queen Mother Hetephis with her ladies and As'enath, Joseph's wife were reassuring poor Galo'Ralao, taking turns with his new scope. Royal brothers, sisters, cousins and spouses. Of course the faithful Butler with his graying head still attached firmly. General Abdu'ra too.

Khufu spoke aloud, "HEAR My People, I Am Khufu! I Am Chosen! I Shall Feed You And Cloth You! I Shall Provide You Cities!" His strong voice boomed off the side of The Great Pyramid and echoed among the crowds of Egyptians. The people shouted adoration. "Ships will fairy my royal brother with volunteer colonist out the Mediterranean and across the sea to new lands, there they shall enlarge the Kingdom and build pyramids and prosper. For those that stay we still have six more years of terrible famine, yet, I Have Provided For You." "We Shall Finish

This Great Pyramid! We Shall Build Our Cities! And I Pharaoh Khufu Shall Have Peace On Earth!" "Now go unto Joseph, what he saith unto you, do."

Joseph looked out at the people. More were arriving daily. Soon foreigners would come from many nations as word spread that there was corn in Egypt. Every man would bring money this year but money would fail then they would bring gold and silver and diamonds. And when the famine continued he would buy their animals or land with the necessary corn until many will sell even themselves unto Pharaoh. Raising a hand to shield the eyes and stepping forward next to his young king, Joseph reflected. He was now thirty eight years old, he was Zaph'nathpaane'ah, Governor of Egypt, a father unto Pharaoh, keeper of the great silo. Now Joseph looked over the people towards the north and remembered his other family, did his beloved father yet live? One day soon he knew his brothers must come to buy corn at this Great Pyramid, he would watch for them. Meanwhile the Old Kingdom would survive.

THE END

The Author lives with his wife and son in historic Georgetown Ohio, where General Ulysses S Grant grew up to become 18th President of the United States. Mr. Douglas is a recognized Author and Theorist; also traverses the country as a professional truck driver. He was educated at Hyles Anderson College, Federal Law Enforcement Training Center, Prince Georges CC & Libraries. This Historical-Nonfiction was inspired by an unlikely discovery, that turns out to be extremely likely! All facts and figures in this book have been carefully researched. This book has a wide market from Popular History and Religious Interest to Egypt and Tourism and makes a great gift for the academic or curiosity reader in your life. Your comments are always welcomed.

"Thank you"

THE GREAT PYRAMID MYSTERY

AMAZING NEW DISCOVERY PROVIDES NEW INSIGHT ON ANCIENT EGYPTIAN HISTORY! WRITTEN FOR THE FUN OF RESEARCH AND DISCOVERY, BY STEPHEN S. DOUGLAS!

EASY TO READ AND LEARN FORMAT! DISCOVER THE EVENT FOR YOURSELF! CONNECT EGYPT'S GREAT PYRAMID TO THE BIBLE'S GREAT FAMINE STORY!

www.ingramcontent.com/pod-product-compliance
Lightning Source LLC
Chambersburg PA
CBHW080935040426
42443CB00015B/3420